The Anatomy
of a
Spiritual Meltdown

The Anatomy of a Spiritual Meltdown

JC Mac

First published 2010
Published in 2010 by My Publishing Company

Copyright © 2010 by JC Mac

ISBN 9781453782415

All rights reserved

The right of JC Mac to be identified as the author of this work has been asserted by him in accordance with the Copyright, Designs and Patents Act 1988.

Typesetting and cover design by www.wordzworth.com

Contents

Foreword	iii
Acknowledgements	ix
A Note On Terminology	xi

Part 1: The Surrender of Existence — 1

Chapter 1: The Dilemma	3
Chapter 2: The Meltdown	5
Chapter 3: Letting Go Versus Holding On	15

Part 2: The Lead Up To 2005 — 23

Chapter 4: The Brother Who Came And Went	25
Chapter 5: Playing Roulette	33
Chapter 6: The Green Shelby	39
Chapter 7: Home On The Range	49
Chapter 8: Mexico Magic	57
Chapter 9: Crazy Horse	68
Chapter 10: Final Comments	78

Foreword

By Dr Larry Culliford

Before turning into gold, base metal needs melting down. JC Mac here gives a vivid, intensely personal and extremely readable account of his own transformation: from chaos to calm, from delinquency and disrespect to wisdom, compassion and love. All the more convincing and moving for being told without sentimentality or self-pity, this remarkable tale holds lessons for us all.

***

A man in his forties once came to my psychiatric consulting room seeking help. He was an expert on information technology heading a small team working in banks and the business industry, keeping the computers running and the information (about shares trading, for example) up to date, minute by minute. It was a high pressure job that he took pride in doing to perfection. One day, a big problem arose with the computers of one of his customers. He was obliged to move into their offices, working round the clock for three days to get it fixed. He was exhausted afterwards, but set about carrying on as before.

A few weeks later, to his dismay, the computer whizz developed a severe skin complaint. It was a form of dermatitis affecting the whole body, making his hands in particular thickened and scaly, stiff and sore. The most devastating effect involved being unable to use the computer keyboard at the required speed. Skin specialists offered creams, ointments and advice, but nothing worked. Desperate to resume working, the man became deeply unhappy.

As often happens, nature had provided with exquisite precision a complaint that forced this man to take a prolonged break from an occupation that, although he could not see and accept it, had been damaging him, using up his vital energy, burning him out. He told me he was, *'having a nervous breakdown'*, but this is not the most helpful description. He needed to see that something else was going on.

Focused for so long almost entirely on his work, neglecting his wife and family as a result, the man's life no longer had any meaning. He was suffering from symptoms of depression, but underlying this, requiring urgent attention, was a profound spiritual problem. His values and attitudes needed revision. There were things he needed to let go of, the very things he was trying so hard to hang onto. In order to heal, to become whole again, he needed to grow.

Problematically, though, he was so driven by the materialistic values involved in high finance and his role in it, that he was not yet ready to change. He did not return after his initial consultation; but perhaps later (after the situation had got worse, no doubt) reflecting again on his predicament, he may have understood something of his need – and the opportunity this illness provided – to let go, to seek personal growth, become emotionally resilient and thereby more spiritually mature.

***

The idea of a breakdown suggests that a person is nothing else than a piece of machinery that has gone wrong, that cannot be fixed without expert external intervention. Call the plumber, the mechanic, the surgeon or the psychiatrist! But this denies nature's own methods of healing and recovery, whether the injury is to flesh, muscle and bone, to the mind, to relationships, or deeper, at the level of the soul. The biological, psychological, social and spiritual dimensions of being human are seamlessly inter-linked. It makes no sense to pay attention to only one or other without considering the whole person. The words 'heal', 'whole' (and 'holy') are also connected, sharing a common root.

I prefer to think of episodes like these not as 'breakdowns' but 'shake-ups', in that they give us important chances to examine, re-shuffle and re-deal at least some of the cards in our hands (the circumstances, values and goals of our lives), refresh ourselves and begin again.

The critical clash, very often, is between worldly, ego-driven goals – like the illusory 'success-seeking' JC describes driving his early life – and more mature spiritual ambitions: to have a meaningful life; to be of use and service to one's fellow human beings, to nature and the planet; and to achieve these by discovering and holding to some kind of sacred worldview.

Many medical practitioners, psychiatrists and psychologists, however, stick with the idea of breakdown. For them, 'mental illness' is just a form of biological and psychological dysfunction. Using this approach, the assessment process leads to 'diagnosis', and diagnosis leads to 'treatment', usually with medication and/or brief psychological therapy. There is nothing wrong with this as far as it goes, and many people benefit, experience 'symptom relief', and get more or less successfully back to their former lifestyle. Many other people, however, do not feel properly listened to, and do not improve very much.

Increasing numbers of professionals in health care and mental health care have therefore been forced to reconsider these failures, and are becoming aware that nature's own healing potential is being ignored. Priceless opportunities are being missed; not only for a more complete (holistic) form of healing, but also for valuable personal development.

Medicine and psychiatry are now, at last, beginning to acknowledge the wisdom of assessing and assisting with people's spiritual needs. The condition of 'spiritual emergence' (sometimes presenting as a 'spiritual *emergency*'), which mimics but is distinguishable from an episode of psychosis, and which should be treated and handled quite differently, is being recognised and written up. Nevertheless, all too often, as *The Anatomy of a Spiritual Meltdown* makes clear, "Conventional medicine has very little to offer". JC Mac was very clear that what was happening to him, "Was spiritual not medical", and, "Required a spiritual solution". I take the view that all four dimensions – biological, psychological, social and spiritual – need taking into account. I do not rule out the value of medical treatments and psychotherapy, but they cannot and must not be the whole story.

The key phenomena associated with spiritual emergence can involve powerful physical and emotional experiences, ever-shifting in form and intensity. As JC discovered, they are frequently painful and emotionally traumatic, but they are not always as frightening. The principal emotions may also include calmness and bliss. Either way, the experience of spiritual emergence is disorientating; and may well feel like a meltdown; so that life simply cannot go on in quite the same way as before.

JC also discovered that a lengthy period of adjustment may be necessary. People need time. They also need basic care and a secure, stress-free, nurturing environment. Furthermore, they need reassurance and guidance as they 'let go' of much of the old and re-integrate their personalities at a new, more conscious, more 'in the moment' level. It involves necessarily and intuitively adopting different, wiser, more compassionate values and objectives, embarking not *towards* a future… but *into* the present… This is now! This is it! This is all there is! All there is, is here, right now! These are the essential insights of enlightenment.

JC expresses brilliantly the many paradoxes involved in this new worldview, employing the kind of humour and humility that prove to me he is the genuine article, a spiritually mature person. He says that the kind of major shift in consciousness he went through requires a high level of support; but adds sadly that, "Here in the West there really isn't any".

This is true. Science and technology, competition and a consumerist culture, have advanced human material wealth and comfort for many, but at the price of neglecting something vital: a spiritual worldview to make sense of, inform and influence our lives, both privately and throughout society.

Both separately and together, then, we need to re-discover and proclaim widely our spiritual nature. JC Mac is one of the pioneers leading the way. His contribution; both selfless and courageous, through the soul-searching and effort needed to write this book;

deserves the gratitude of all going through similar trials, who will undoubtedly come to treasure it as a precious source of encouragement, inspiration and hope.

It is true that there are few conventional answers or straightforward formulae here. "The world we live in is truly a mystery", says JC. "The more I know, the less I know, and that's all I know." But there are many useful pointers in a series of breath-taking vignettes from his almost impossibly adventurous life on why, and how, to let go; on allowing the false and foolish 'everyday ego' to quiet down, leaving the soul to take control, letting the true 'spiritual self', intuitively attuned to an indescribable higher level of sacred unity (that some people refer to simply as 'God'), guard and guide our thoughts, words and actions.

JC's take on it goes like this: "There is God's will and then there is our will. Take a wild guess which one works better when it comes to having things turn out well in life". His many tales – of major losses and facing death, of magical happenings and meaningful coincidences – tell of confronting his attachments, his anger and his fear, over and over again, until he is gradually able to let go of them all.

In remarking unflinchingly that we too must eventually die, JC reminds us that life sets us all the same test paper. Also, however much or little we amass in between, we start with nothing and leave with nothing. This fact alone should teach us something; but, as he says, we have usually been conditioned to ignore it, to live as if we will never die. This is the pre-condition for meltdown; so, when reality does break through our defences to strike us, naturally we are knocked sideways and feel it badly. Ouch! The message is, we should be better prepared.

The knowledge of our death lies within us; in our frail and vulnerable bodies and in our intelligent souls. Reminders are everywhere too. Pick up a newspaper! Watch the news! For however long and however successfully we continue to ignore it, somehow it keeps coming back. The way forward, as JC demonstrates repeatedly, is to accept the inevitability of fate and go beyond self-centredness.

Surprisingly, life becomes richer and more meaningful, rather than less. Only when prepared to die well are we really ready to live well. When you understand that everything is on loan and basically you have nothing, then you are free… because you have nothing to lose.

At first it's bewildering, even scary, but JC Mac does us the favour of making this ultimately inescapable journey sound safe, even fun, and decidedly worthwhile. His book is wonderfully entertaining. It's superbly educational… And it's hard to put down.

Larry Culliford

Sussex, UK
6th August 2010

Dr Larry Culliford, a Consultant Psychiatrist in the NHS for over twenty years, helped found the 'Spirituality and Psychiatry' special interest group of the Royal College of Psychiatrists. He is the author of *Love, Healing and Happiness: Spiritual Wisdom for Secular Times* (O Books, 2007) and *The Psychology of Spirituality: An Introduction* (Jessica Kingsley Publishers, Nov 2010).

Acknowledgements

This book could not have been written if it were not for my three children, Matthew, James and Jessica. In my darkest moments, when all seemed lost and the free fall through the endless pit of hell was never ending, their presence gave me the strength to carry on.

To my mother and father, for doing everything they could in the face of insurmountable odds. To my brothers and sisters, for being such a huge influence in what I have become. To my Aunt Penny and the support she has provided throughout our families' lives. To the band of brothers whom I grew up with in the streets of America and Canada, especially 'the crew' and all its fallen, who lived and died with me in the 'projects,' also known as 'The Valley.' Their memories will remain forever with me; their loyalty was unwavering.

To Evan Renaerts, the first man to never judge me, for pointing the way towards the 'Fire of Zen' and the possibility of redemption. To all the great men from 'the firm' who have mentored me over the last twenty-five years and for the unwavering support they continually provide for me. I would be lost without them. To Mitch and Bobby, who to this day remain two of my best friends. To the military, for showing me the meaning of true leadership and honor. To Paul Taylor, for his friendship and integrity when it comes to standing on the firing line of life. To the crew I work with at Alkoomi Ltd.; their belief in me has allowed my gift to make a difference in the world. To Clothilde, for her continued support and love during the writing of this book.

To all those who were there during the collapse of the ego and the support they provided during my integration back into the world of form. To all the earthly angels who continually re-sparked my faith, reassuring me that the journey towards the last door was near, and all that was required was to continually surrender moment to moment, until, finally, the divine light of God burst through unannounced, stunning and indescribable. And finally, for all those who still suffer while trapped in the illusion of separation.

I love you all.

JC Mac

A Note On Terminology

GOD: I use the term God in the broadest sense of the word, simply as a means of including everyone in the conversation. You may be more comfortable with other terminology, such as the universe, the divine, a higher power, your higher mind and so on. You do not have to believe in anything to derive value from the information in this book. All that is required is an open mind and the willingness to see things in a different way.

DUALITY: You will come across this word repeatedly throughout this book. Duality means living with a sense of self that is separate from others. It is the perception of the world of form, the mind, verbal communication, right and wrong, up and down, good and bad. It exists as a 'real illusion' at a certain level of consciousness.

LINEAR and NON-LINEAR REALITY: These terms are just another way of speaking about duality and the state of non-duality, or one might say the perception of opposites as mentioned above; the visible and invisible and so on. Opposites exist in the linear world. In the non-linear world, all is one; all exists as a part of everything else.

THE EGO: The ego develops in early childhood when we realize that we are separate entities from our parents and carers. A healthy sense of self, or ego, is, of course, not a bad thing. It is the basic psychological structure we need to function effectively in the world of duality and to relate well with others; it is how we know where we stop and others begin. Yet, at the same time, the ego can be the cause of endless suffering.

As we grow up and try to 'become somebody' in a dual world of opposites, the ego-self strives to achieve and goes into competition with others. It likes to look good, win and be right about all things. All conflict, both with others and within yourself, is driven by the competitive ego-mind seeking more and more out of life. It is the ego that drives the endless mind chatter about our lives, the filter between you and your true nature. It has no interest in giving up its position, nor having you transcend its trap during the journey towards enlightenment. It is a double-edged sword.

CONSCIOUSNESS: This is what one might say is your true nature. When experienced it occurs as a loving infinite, living, still, silent field of awareness, timeless and without form or space. It is the big 'I' behind the ego-based little 'I.' In a state of pure consciousness there are no longer any distinctions or labels. Nothing is separate. You are it and it is you. It is *what* you are, not who you are.

KARMA: This is an Eastern term and describes what we know in the West as cause and effect. It states that whatever we do comes with a consequence, both good and bad. Every thought, every deed, every action we take in life influences the infinite field of consciousness, resulting in setting up the conditions of one's life. A point that must be made clear is that good karma does not lead to enlightenment; as enlightenment is not caused by anything happening.

PART 1

The Surrender Of Existence

*"Other people have what they need; I alone possess nothing.
I alone drift about, like someone without a home.
I am like an idiot, my mind is so empty."*

The Tao

CHAPTER 1

The Dilemma

Right from the start, we have got an impediment. This book requires a linear, rational mind to read it, and what I am trying to convey is a non-linear topic. It is not a concept, but a direct experience.

For example, you can look up the concept of 'cat' in the dictionary. You can read the description, maybe even a few books on the subject of cats. You can study for a Ph.D. in feline behavior, but it still doesn't give you access to what it is to be a cat. Only a cat knows that. (I'm a poet and didn't know it.) The same goes with advancement in spiritual states. If, one day, out of the blue, you happen to transcend the conceptual mind of duality, you are going to have a tough time explaining that experience to someone who has not.

I have been running into this dilemma since 2005, when, as you will read later on, my mind and ego-self literally vanished. As much as I think I can actually communicate my experience to others, I am often left wondering whether it is even worth it, or if people are actually interested. I sometimes think it might be better if I just stopped talking about it altogether and got on with my life.

So let me pre-empt this book by saying that some of the material you come across cannot be explained or understood by the mind. How does one explain the unexplainable? In fact, the more you try to understand this material in a rational manner, the more confusing it may become, and the further from the fundamental point you may drift. For that I apologize and ask you to forgive my lack of linear skill in this matter. There are no words that can describe the sheer power of the reality of God's love when one is confronted with it, face to face. It is one thing to read books and manuscripts about God. It is another thing altogether to sit across the table and have a large latte in the presence of that kind of power.

The reason for this phenomenon is that the mind and ego act like a filter between you and the truth of reality. What the mind sees depends upon how that filter has been set up. As long as those filters are there, you cannot see reality as it is. When the mind appears, reality disappears. It is crucial to understand the difference; it is the *way* you look at things that determines what you see, and the way you see is set up by these so-called filters. All of this is contingent on one's level of consciousness.

What we are actually seeing is what I call 'a real illusion of reality.' It looks, feels and smells absolutely real – but it isn't!

The mind is part of the world of form and content, and is the wrong apparatus to try and access spirit and the non-linear. As the saying goes: 'The mind is a great servant but a terrible master.' Having said all that, this mind of ours is one of the only tools we have in the beginning of our spiritual journey to try and understand consciousness and the realization of enlightenment. So, it looks like we are left in a bit of a quandary.

My advice then, is to just go ahead and use that beautiful mind that God gave you to read what is on these pages. I would also advise not spending a lot of time trying to figure it all out; just let it wash over you. At a much deeper level, it really doesn't matter whether your mind figures it out or not. Your essential self (the one beyond the ego) already knows everything I am about to share with you. In fact, what you may experience is simply a sense of remembering something you had forgotten, a long, long time ago.

There is only one truth, and that truth rings true for us all when we experience it. So, let reading this book be both a linear and a non-linear experience. I invite you to enjoy the mental process of reading it and also the silent stillness whence it came. Enjoy the paradox, as I continually contradict myself.

CHAPTER 2

The Meltdown

"Holding on is your will. Letting go is God's will."
JC Mac

The most crucial and profound moment in the whole of my life was when I was suddenly confronted with what I thought was about to be my own death. Was I to trust and let go into the unknown? Or was I going to fearfully hold on until the bitter end?

It was August 15, 2005, a normal working day for me in my home office. As I was hanging up the phone after speaking to a business client, suddenly, and for no apparent reason, I began to cry and could not stop. A strong sensation, similar to that of pins and needles and rushing water, began to move down through the top of my head and up through my arms and legs. I tried to shake it off but it would not leave me. Instead, it just got stronger and stronger. At first, I thought it might have been because I had been sitting in my chair for too long. Maybe my body had fallen asleep, or my circulation had been cut off. Whatever the reason, the sensation continued to build.

Within what seemed like only a few moments I felt as if I was under a massive waterfall. I was unable to move as the weight of the 'water' pounded my body and beat me to the ground. The experience became so intense that I ended curled up on the floor in the fetal position, terrified that I was about to die from either a heart attack or a stroke. After all I had accomplished throughout my life, I thought to myself, here I was now, about to die alone and bewildered on the floor. What had happened to my fantasy of going out in a blaze of glory?

As the fear of death consumed me, I began thinking about just how long it was going to take for the end to arrive. How painful was it going to be when I left this body? Was there a god who would judge me as having lived a good life? Was I destined for heaven, or wherever good boys go? Or had my self-centered existence sealed my fate in hell?

As I lay there on the floor, I could feel myself becoming paralyzed. Every part of me began to ache; it felt like every bone in my body was about to break. I moaned in agony as I rolled around on the floor, my arms and legs stiff and frozen from the force of the energy rushing through me. I had never really spent much time during my life thinking about what it might be like in that final moment. Now that it had arrived, I realized I was completely unprepared for it. I was at the absolute mercy of whatever was coming next.

In tears and terrified, I managed to crawl to the phone and attempt to call for help. It was almost impossible to dial the number because the pain in my hands was so intense. Eventually, however, I got through to my close friend Evan. After a few moments he told me that what was happening sounded more like a spiritual experience than a medical emergency. By now, my hands were so badly cramped that they stopped working, and the phone fell and landed next to my head. As I tried to keep speaking to my friend, I noticed that his voice was beginning to fade into the distance. The sensation of rushing water was now sending the noise of the normal, linear world far into the background.

Whilst lying there overwhelmed by the fear of death, a passage from a Zen Buddhist text I had once read crossed my mind: 'All fear is illusion. Walk straight ahead.' In a last desperate attempt to somehow save myself, I began praying. I chanted the words: 'In the name of the highest good, Thy will be done,' over and over. Then, a moment of clarity came. I realized I had a choice. The first one was to hang on to my life for all it was worth, right up until the bitter end, in a desperate attempt to stay alive. The other option was to let go and trust in God and whatever was in store for me. I could see that I had no control over what was taking place. So I let go of existence itself, and trusted in the unknown.

Within moments, I felt like someone was wrapping a thick warm blanket around me on a cold night. It was like a profound presence was somehow communicating to me that everything was going to be alright, and to just let go and continue to surrender to what was taking place.

So surrender I did, and like a set of falling dominos, I let go of my attachment to everything I thought was real in my life. First my physical body, then the mind and all its thoughts, feeling, opinions, assessments and positions; my children, my business career, the house, the car, my friends, the fear and terror of the unknown and, finally, all I had accomplished during my short stay here on this beautiful planet. I was now ready to die in peace and acceptance.

Then as quickly and powerfully as the raging spiritual hurricane had battered my little shell of a body into the ground, it vanished. The voice in my head disappeared and everything went absolutely silent and utterly still. As I looked up from the floor, I could see what I can only describe as a living electromagnetic field of love, emanating from everything.

Was I dreaming? Had I died and gone to heaven? And if so, was someone coming to meet me at the gates? Did I pass the test?

I then noticed there was no separation between me and everything else in the room. The table, the chairs, the rug, even what I thought was my body... everything seemed to be part of the same unified thing; part of this field of love that I had been catapulted into. I was overwhelmed with a peace beyond anything one could ever imagine, 'a peace which passeth all understanding.' In the presence of such indescribably exquisite bliss, all I could do was cry.

The world of duality, time and location had disappeared unannounced. What seemed like movement, stopped. It became clear that nothing had any more – or less – importance than anything else. There were no longer any hierarchy or labels to the form of life. I could see myself in everything and everything shone back to me with equal power and radiance; everything vibrated with the energy of life itself. All things were in a state of absolute perfection.

It then occurred to me that a lifetime of desire, and the need for achievement and success, had disappeared too. The identity I had created over a lifetime of thinking had simply vanished. Who I thought I was, how I related to life, all my accomplishments, were now gone. Although I was aware I had a body, looking at it was just like looking at a piece of furniture; or at a toy that now moved under some kind of guiding force. Rather than identify with my body, I now simply observed it walking, talking and moving around the apartment.

There was no longer a personal 'I.' No longer a 'me' looking at a 'you.' Doing had been replaced by 'being.' The noise of life faded into the background and was replaced by an utterly profound, infinite peace, stillness and silence. This new dimension became my new reality.

The beauty of this state was so intense that I continued to cry almost every day for the next year.

Being catapulted so directly and unexpectedly into this profound stillness made it very hard for me to function, or, indeed, do anything at all. Even the smallest of tasks became cumbersome and difficult. There were long periods when I could not eat, wash, move – or even speak. I became unshaven, pale and lost so much weight; my clothes began to hang off me. I remember passing the mirror one day and wondering who this skinny person was in the apartment with me. It took a few moments to recognize what I was now looking at – one might say it was the body formerly known as me that was now walking around the house.

Leaving the apartment became almost impossible. I found myself just sitting for hours on end, catatonic. During this time, my son once paid me a visit, just to then point out to me that I was actually drooling. My reply was: "Son, get used to it."

You could say I was in a state of exquisite shock. A whole lifetime of endless thoughts, opinions, self-criticism, evaluation and assessment of myself and my place in the world no longer existed. It was extraordinary to realize how much stress this relentless internal monologue creates – and how it separates us from life itself.

THE ANATOMY OF A SPIRITUAL MELTDOWN

After almost a year of being in this blissfully mindless state, I tried to get back into the world by taking walks. I would manage to make my way to the local shops where I would sit for hours on end, watching people going about their daily business. One day, while walking through the bread section in my local supermarket, I noticed yet again that everything was in a profound state of perfection. All things (form) became utterly sacred. The bread aisle of Sainsbury's had suddenly transformed into a temple of divine eternal beauty. The experience was so overwhelming that all I could do was stand there, stunned, as tears of gratitude streamed down my face.

I must have looked like one of those disheveled old men who shuffle around in their slippers to the shops, looking completely lost. The kind of person many of us silently laugh at as a 'care in the community' case, living on state benefits. Goodness knows what the other shoppers thought of this scruffy, middle-aged man in floods of tears, while they cautiously reached over me for a French stick and bag of rolls. Eventually the manager appeared and gently escorted me out of the store. (Life's embarrassing, then you die).

***

One day I managed to make it out of the apartment to the communal rubbish bins. The area was fenced off and as I opened the gate and walked in, I was struck by the beauty of the waste all around me. I stood there just soaking up the radiance of everything in view. A visit to the bin area was just another opportunity to experience the perfection of all things.

As I wandered around in this state of 'oneness,' feeling overwhelmed with the radiant beauty of life, I would often see people moving along the streets as if they were in some kind of trance, like half-dead zombies in a bad B movie. I could see the internal dialogue on their faces and how lifetimes of thought had literally shaped their bodies and the circumstances of their lives.

I realized that nothing was actually 'happening.' Whatever did emerge was only as a result of a certain set of conditions. Just like when it rains it can only do so when all the conditions needed for rain to happen are in place. Then we witness what the conceptual mind calls and experiences as rain.

I needed very little food or sleep and could go for days at a time without any of it. One morning after a light rest, I got up and sat on the edge of the bed. I then suddenly realized that it was dark outside. The whole day had slipped away without any realization of time whatsoever. All I could do was climb back into bed and lay there in the timeless bliss of reality. With the illusion of time and location now shattered, everything was emerging without sequence, beginnings or ends.

When I did get up, walking was difficult. It felt like my body had aged a hundred years. Some days all I could do was make it from the sofa to the hallway. I would find myself standing there in a timeless dimension, gazing at the beauty of the woodwork, or marveling at some other small detail. I had the sense that all objects could actually communicate to me, and that they, also, were somehow aware of my presence.

No matter what I was witnessing, whether it was the stunning architecture of an old cathedral or the town dump, it all radiated the beauty of life with the same vitality. You see, the mind can only function within certain rules and parameters. It needs to label things, put things into time and space, and see life in terms of opposites and from a perspective of separation (a 'you' and a 'me'). When the mind disappears, then the way it operates disappears along with it.

**

Then, about thirteen months into this blissful unity with all things, I began to notice the return of thoughts, judgments and opinions. The more they filled my head, the darker my world became. The still silent awareness that had overtaken my life now started to move into the background once again. As it did, the beautiful, radiant color and profound peace of God went with it.

THE ANATOMY OF A SPIRITUAL MELTDOWN

Looking back, I can clearly see that this was the ego-mind returning, trying to reclaim authorship of my life. The trouble is, when the ego senses its own annihilation, it generates fear. Huge amounts of fear. It marked the beginning of what I can only describe as a journey into the deepest depths of hell; an endless pit of terror. Why had I been abandoned by God, hung out to dry and slung back into the realm of mental suffering? What had I done to deserve such a fate? I felt completely and utterly alone.

I would awake crying at five in the morning, gripped with unknown terror, desperately clutching my six-year-old daughter's teddy bear. This descent into darkness continued to deepen day after day for what seemed like forever. Every morning I would awake into the same terrifying fear and mental isolation until death began to look like a viable option; a way to put an end to all this suffering. It felt like some evil black force that was driving me insane. (The Jedi in me was now losing out to the dark side.) I had been tested many times throughout my life but nothing that could match the power of this place.

I believe it was Dante who wrote the phrase: 'Abandon hope all ye who enter here.' During my darkest days I often wondered if he had been to the same place, whether he had managed to get out – and, if so, how on earth did he do it. I was convinced the darkness was permanent. All my cries for help and prayers for salvation seemed to be falling on deaf ears. This to me was hell at its very worst.

I was alone, lost in the deepest recesses of my mind. I realized my ego would rather throw me off a bridge than surrender to God again.

In desperation I would call out to the one or two people I knew who had some understanding of what I was going through; who had been through spiritual crises of their own. I would weep down the phone to them for hours at a time, terrified to hang up and be left alone with myself once again. When I finally did end the call I would crawl back into bed for another night of terror. I would often awake in the night with what felt like bolts of lightning shooting up my arms. Then that sense of rushing water and pins and needles would begin crashing down upon me again. I was so frightened by this point that I would jump out of bed and shake my limbs in a vain attempt to make it all go away. Not that it ever worked. When I got back into bed the rushing sensation would just slowly begin moving through my body again.

It meant that I went for days at a time without sleep. It was like being electrocuted all the time. The power surges would pound my body relentlessly, seemingly with no concern for me at all. What was left of my mind just could not accept what was happening.

If you do happen to find that one day all thought vanishes forever, then God bless you. Please, enjoy the ride. But if your mind does happen to come back, then good luck. When the ego-self realizes that its days are numbered, it tends to fight back – viciously in my case – and will do anything to hold onto its domain. What it doesn't understand is that it can still keep its job. But the new deal is that it gets demoted from being the C.E.O. of the corporation to the floor sweeper. In my ego's case, that new position was totally unacceptable.

I had unbelievable cravings. I would eat bags of sweets followed by buckets of strong coffee, in an attempt to try and make contact with my body again. None of it ever worked though. I had become an 'it' with no location in time or space, all of which contributed to my ego-mind's sense of complete alienation from life. I could see that this ego was not going to give up so easily. It was putting up the fight of a lifetime, terrified of being obliterated completely.

Many people ask me how I eventually managed to integrate my mind and spirit back into a functioning unity. To tell you the truth, I am not sure myself. I do know, however, that it included every grain of wisdom that I had gleaned from a life of hard knocks and over twenty-five years of personal development and transformational work. This, along with a stint in the army, the training of some of the world's top spiritual and life mentors and the blessing of many of my great friends, helped pull me through during my darkest moments. The path to enlightenment requires true self-leadership.

THE ANATOMY OF A SPIRITUAL MELTDOWN

Today I can see that one needs to be physically, mentally and emotionally fit to even attempt major shifts in consciousness like this. The intensity is such that I would not be surprised to hear that it has killed many people already. As for the support needed afterwards, well, here in the West there isn't really any. There may be in India and places like that but I still believe that, wherever you are, finding the right people to support you can be a difficult and lengthy process. For the most part, you are on your own.

At best you might end up in an institution being medicated up to your eyeballs. Conventional medicine has very little to offer cases like myself, apart from sectioning in a psychiatric ward. I have nothing against the numerous benefits of modern medicine but this approach could lead to much bigger problems later on. The one thing that kept me going was knowing that what was happening to me was spiritual not medical, and that it required a spiritual solution.

Financially things had become bleak. I had by now not been able to work at full capacity in almost two years. I had children, a mortgage, a failed marriage to support plus the rent on my apartment, food, school bills and all the other overheads it takes to function in today's Western world. To this day, I have no idea how some of those costs got paid.

I do remember that at one point my landlady actually lent me two months' rent so she wouldn't have to evict me. I honestly never thought I would work again. For someone who had previously been so relentless at chasing and living the dream – and earning top whack to boot – the sense of hopelessness about my ability to provide just exacerbated my sense of despair.

***

It was during this period that a miracle happened. I got a call offering me the first piece of work I had been given in a long time. Incapable as I had become, I pulled myself together and headed into town to meet a new client. It was a hot August London day. The Underground trains were jam-packed with tourists and people from all walks of life making their journeys across town. As I was jostled onto the train, I could feel the fear and terror descending upon me again. Panic rose in my chest, and all I could think about was how the hell I was going to get out of the carriage so I could breathe again.

Then suddenly I felt the warm touch of someone's hand in mine. Startled, I looked down to see a beautiful little girl, about seven years old. She had mistaken my hand for that of her father's, the man standing next to me. She never looked up but the feel of that hand in mine was like a blessing from an angel, one who had come down from heaven to let me know that everything was going to be alright; and even though this was my darkest hour, I was being carried. It was as if God was saying: "I know I am kicking your ass here JC, but trust me. Surrender to it all, and I will carry you."

This was the turning point. A new sense of power and confidence came over me; and things began to change for the better. Bit by bit, with every day that passed, the sense of fear and despair began to lift. Slowly, I began to feel human again. I started getting out more and telling people about my experience. I scoured the internet, asking if anyone knew of other people who had been through the same kind of experience as mine. I visited spiritual communities looking for anyone who I could relate to. Anyone who could sit with me and say: 'Yes. I have been there. This is what you can expect; and this is what you can do to manage your way to wholeness again.'

It took me over four years to find a balance between the world of form and the formless bliss of divinity. It is only now many years later that I can look back in clarity and bring you my experience in a way that I hope deepens your sense of peace and serenity in life.

I am told that there are no mistakes in God's world. My journey has been my journey. Yours, I am certain, will be different. I wish you a gentle and empowering transition into the light.

CHAPTER 3

Letting Go Versus Holding On

"Enlightenment emerges in the practice of surrender and letting go."
JC Mac

When I look back over my life, I can see now that so much of it was about learning to let go. All the successes and failures, all the people, places and worldly experiences I had notched up on my belt, had brought me to that final door; that definitive moment when it dawned on me that I was about to leave my body and that there was no way back.

During my life I have had guns pointed at my head, smashed cars up, been in bar room brawls, lived homeless in the streets of North America, had bikers beating my door down looking for their money and seen many people die from drug and alcohol addiction. I have survived many dangerous situations. None of them, however, matched that terrifying moment that took place on August 15, 2005.

Looking back I can clearly see the process that I went through the moment I thought I was about to die. First there was an unwillingness to accept what was happening, like a kind of denial. Then a deep sense of fear and terror began to settle in, followed by an overwhelming feeling of sadness and loss for all the things that I had not accomplished during my time on the planet. No way was I ready to go.

Could it be that God had gotten his timing wrong? Surely what was happening was meant for someone else. (I mean, don't we all think that everyone else will go before us and that we will be the last one out?) Certainly not for this funny, confident, talented, middle-aged guy who, he believed, was just really beginning to get a handle on things; whose career was on the brink of greatness and accomplishment. There was a profound sense that something was wrong and that the universe had seriously screwed up.

I had lived my life like it was going to continue forever. These things happened to other people. When it came to me I had assumed I was invincible; there was nothing I couldn't do if I put my mind to it: Success in business, relationships, being a soldier, wealth, surviving years in the street and making it out alive when many others had not. I thought I was 'bulletproof.' I thought I had been given the keys to the kingdom.

Denial is a tricky thing because when you are in it, you are blind to it – and once you notice you are in it, then suddenly you are out of it. The trick is to find some way to get the hell out of it before you look back and notice you missed the whole trip. Mix this in with a dose of arrogance and complacency and you have the story of my life. If there is one thing I have learned, it is that not many of us are looking forward to our last moment here on earth. None of us wakes up in the morning in a deep meditative state contemplating how we are going to respond to the moment of our own death.

One of the reasons I believe we all want to avoid this topic is because we are ignorant about the facts. We are ignorant about what is really happening, not only during our lives but also at that final moment and beyond. Everyone I know, including myself, who has seen loved ones die, or has suddenly been confronted with that reality themselves, experiences a deep sense of fear and loss. My assertion is that this fear comes from ignorance about the way life works. That doesn't mean we don't mourn the loss of our loved ones. Of course we do. It means we can learn to mourn with the power of truth in our lives instead of feeling victimized by it.

Now given that all life is impermanent, that all of us are on the way out and we are all going to be confronted with that last moment just before we leave this earthly realm, it might just be worth knowing how things work. I firmly believe that what you decide to do at that moment will depend on how much you have practiced the truth during your life.

THE ANATOMY OF A SPIRITUAL MELTDOWN

Let me explain. When we hold onto life it is an affirmation of fear and a lack of trust in the process. Holding onto something that is impermanent can only lead to upset and suffering at some point. Yet even though we may know this at some level, we still cling to life and many of the things in it. We cling to our possessions, our bodies, relationships, careers and families. We hold on in the wish and hope that nothing will go wrong, or that any of it will be taken from us. Life only feels finite when you are confronted with losing it. Death brings clarity.

Now don't get me wrong. If we were terrified of life all the time we would never get out of bed. But I am not talking about that kind of thing. What I am talking about is facing the fear of letting go; and the best way to face that fear is to know how the game of life is played and how life works. Because then and only then does one have real choice, power and trust in the matter.

If we send a message of fear and lack of trust into the field of consciousness at the moment of death, it influences the conditions that affect what happens next. Why? Because in an infinite universe that is made up of pure consciousness and is highly influenced by every thought, deed and act, the power of one thought can shift the direction and destiny of one's whole life in the blink of an eye. In fact, your destiny just changed by reading this paragraph. Enlightenment is completely contingent on what you think and do. In the end you are on your own; there is no one waiting at the gate when you approach. The final surrender is between you and God, and the access to that meeting is based on conditions.

Think of it this way. When the sun shines, for example, it is because a set of conditions are appropriate for the sun to emerge at that moment. This principle applies to all things, including us. That is why I say that the choice you make at that final moment can determine the direction of what happens next. Your choice influences the conditions. Although it is not the whole story, it certainly plays a big part in one's overall karmic destiny. Holding on sets you moving in one direction; letting go moves you in another.

So, let's look at letting go, the difference it makes to your life and also the power it holds for you in your final moment. When you let go you are saying: 'Everything is OK. Things are as they should be. I am safe. God is with me.' There is a catch, however, as letting go takes practice, just like everything else in life does. But when you can let go, it sends a completely different message into the field of infinite consciousness; one, as I have said, that influences whatever happens next.

Don't just take my word for it. Look at your own experience. How many times have you been attached to something, even worshipped it, and then lost it? How did that make you feel? Did you suffer? Then look at the times when you have been willing and able to walk away from something, unconcerned whether you lose it or not. Now, tell me, which approach gives you more power and freedom in life?

I believe that most of us spend most of our time holding on. We do this because no one ever taught us the benefit of letting go. I don't remember taking 'Letting Go 101' in college, do you? Through sheer ignorance of the truth – and all our cultural taboos about facing death, grief and loss – we learn to grasp and cling to the many places, people and things that we believe give our lives meaning and value.

As I mentioned earlier, I have spent much, if not all, of my life with the underlying assumption that I am going to live forever. Now that I am moving well into my fifties I am beginning to see that the end is much closer than the beginning. I have been brought up in the West where matters of mortality are rarely spoken about. Most of us are completely unprepared for the loss of our loved ones – and even more unprepared for our own exit. So, knowing that we all suffer from a lack of education on the topic of life and death, I understand why we automatically hold on as tight as we possibly can, in the insane belief that we can stop the process of life and our inevitable demise. It does not matter how much plastic surgery you have done, how many vitamins you take or how often you go to the gym. You and I are all ageing and moving closer and closer to our final moment. Being unable to accept that process means we suffer.

THE ANATOMY OF A SPIRITUAL MELTDOWN

In reality everything, including you, is in a state of perfection at every stage of existence. It is our false perceptions caused by our current state of consciousness that set up this delusion that ageing and death is a bad thing; that it is imperfect. Instead of facing the truth, we invent things like the beauty and cosmetic industry to try and deal with our delusions. In the long run, this can only lead to more suffering. The closer you are to the truth, the more peace and unity you experience with everything around you and the more effective you are in life. The further away from the truth you are, the more you suffer.

I really did think I was dying on the floor of my apartment that day in 2005. I can still, to this day, clearly remember how it happened. Everything began to slow down and, as it did, I could see my unwillingness to let go and trust in the process of what was happening. It was only after what seemed like a lifetime of terror and fear for the loss of my existence here on this planet that my many years of personal and spiritual development kicked in – and opened up the possibility of a choice. Was I going to hold on or let go? In those few seconds what arose was a level of trust and faith that I was being taken care of. It was because of this insight that I chose to surrender to the power I had, over many years, come to believe in.

I also want to point out that nothing of what I am advocating is provable in any way by the mind, science or technology. In fact, the more you use those tools, the further away from the truth you move. Linear tools do not work when navigating the non-linear world. Science cannot give you access to the spirit. This is because science is of the mind and the world of form. Spirit, meanwhile, is the world of the formless. There is an old saying: 'You cannot think your way to heaven.' In fact, you cannot even experience it until you transcend the mind. Try not to think about that… Just kidding.

So, we could say life is a process of letting go; and the longer you live, the more there is to let go of. So the better you get at surrender, the easier the journey is going to be. I also want you to keep in mind that when one does let go they always do so from the present moment. It is impossible to let go from the future or the past. I say this because letting go cannot take place in a linear, sequential timeline. It is not a function of the mind but of the spirit, which is timeless and has no location in reality.

What makes people crazy is trying to think 'letting go.' This is like a fish with a hook in its mouth. The harder it tries to get away the deeper the hook sinks in. So the more you think, the further away you move from the truth. Most of us become willing to let go through the sheer agony of continuing to hold on.

Just as repetition is the mother of skill, letting go takes practice. The better you get at it, the more peace you experience and the less you suffer. When we can be in this moment, free of the trappings of the past and future, knowing there is never anything wrong, we have an honest shot at giving it all up. With that knowledge comes the confidence that it is safe to surrender. I love the idea that whatever is happening is exactly what is supposed to be happening at that moment. The reason that is true is in the simple fact that it is happening. Everything at every moment is normal for that moment. How could it be otherwise?

This book could be looked at in many ways: As a guide to peaceful living, or a study on the practice of living in the moment. Or how about seeing it as a book on improving your mental, emotional and, therefore, physical health? The one that drives it home for me, more than anything else, is to see it as a book on living a great life, by learning how to surrender and let go, moment to moment. Learn how to let go and you learn how to live.

So, with your permission, I would like to tell you a few stories from my life, the ones that I think contributed to setting up the conditions that took place in 2005. They are the tales of how I have stumbled through life and, along the way, learned the skill of letting go, through the fine art of screwing everything up all the time. I want to share with you my journey and how, in hindsight, those lessons became great teachers; how they have taught me to let go with less and less struggle and suffering.

So please take this journey with me. Take what you can from what I have to offer and use it to improve the quality of your own life right now. Even more importantly, use it to prepare yourself for your entry through that last door, at that last moment. Remember, nobody gets out alive. The clock continues to tick for each and every one of us. If I had the choice between education and wisdom I would pick wisdom hands down. Education is the process of learning through repetition while wisdom comes from experience and is often born out of some of our biggest mistakes.

PART 2

The Lead Up To 2005

*"The fastest way to enlightenment
is to screw everything up all the time."*

JC Mac

CHAPTER 4

The Brother Who Came And Went

*"The mind is like a thief.
It has spent eons mastering the art of robbing you of this very moment."*

JC Mac

When I was four years old my family left England to set up a new life in Canada. It was 1957 and the British Empire was looking for people who were interested in beginning a new life in this far off British colony. My father had finished his career in football and decided that a new start meant a new life. So we sailed off to this new land and ended up moving into a little square wooden box of a house in Toronto. I remember a distinct sense of possibility in the air, not only for us, but also for the many others who had made the journey to this distant land.

Brian was the firstborn, followed by my sister Teresa. Then I came along and so did Peter, Jane and Katie. We had just a couple of bedrooms, a coal fire and a small backyard that my brothers and I used to turn into an ice rink during the cold Canadian winter months. Though we never had much we were all happy with life.

All us kids slept in the same room, which meant it took forever for our worn out parents to get us off to sleep. I can still hear my dad screaming: "Go to bed!" It never worked though. We just laughed and kept on playing. The summers were hot and the winters were cold but that never mattered to us. We all loved running around outside, no matter what the weather. I can remember walking home from school in the blistering cold with my older brother Brian, our clothes soaking wet from all the playing in the snow banks.

We would get home and warm ourselves by the coal fire while watching the little black and white TV we had at the time. Wow, how that has all changed. I now struggle to drag my kids away from their

Game Boys, PlayStations, computers and the 150 digital TV channels they now have. In those days there were no Starbucks, Costa Coffee, mobile phones, wireless internet connection and all the rest of our modern day technology. No. My mom would throw us outside in the morning and we would pile back home in the afternoon, worn out from playing with our friends throughout the neighborhood.

Brian was the oldest and we all looked up to him. As the first-born he held high rank in the family food chain and was adored by both my parents. As we all got a little older we began finding our own friends, but would still run into each other as we all hung out in the same neighborhood. In those days, you could walk in and out of anyone's home on our street and be guaranteed a free meal. At times you could even be disciplined by other parents who lived on the block. I can recall stepping out of line one day and being yelled at by a friend's father. Upon telling my parents what happened they told me that I probably deserved it. And you know what? I did. Try that in this day and age of media-driven fear and paranoid parents. I can't even take photos of my kids playing football in the school playground without a teacher running up to me, thinking I'm some kind of a perverted nut. Wow, God help us all.

The older we all got, the closer we became as a family. It was great having so many brothers and sisters in the house even if the house was small. There was always something to do or someone to play with. A few years ago an old buddy of mine posted me (not emailed – can you believe it?) a couple of old photos of our old house in Toronto. It was so tiny! I couldn't get my head around how we all managed to squeeze ourselves into that little matchbox of a house – and live there so happily.

Just as things couldn't get any better, Brian went up to my mom one day and complained of sores in his mouth. I don't think my parents thought much about it at first but he continued to talk about how painful the sores were. Finally they took him to the doctor's to see what the problem was. Us kids never heard much about what transpired during that visit. I think there was a period of waiting to hear what was going on. When the test results arrived, the

THE ANATOMY OF A SPIRITUAL MELTDOWN

doctor told my parents to take Brian straight to hospital. So my mom packed up his things and off they went.

In my head everything was going to be fine. Whatever the problem was the hospital would sort it out and he would be back to his old self in a flash. We would pick up where we left off and go back to having fun and living our lives. But that's not how it worked out. After a week had passed and Brian still wasn't home, I began to wonder what was going on.

I learned much later on that my mom and dad were up at the hospital every day sitting by his bed in support of what was happening. Just the look on their faces when they would walk through the door at night told me that something wasn't right. But they said he was having more tests done and that he was fine. In fact, my mom would bring home drawings and pictures Brian had been making for us from his hospital bed to let us know he was doing OK.

Then one morning a few weeks into this ordeal, my dad sat us all down on the sofa. I could see my mom at the kitchen table, silent and pale. The look on their faces pretty much said it all. In disbelief I heard my dad say that my hero and big brother Brian had died that night of a blood disease called leukemia. From the day of his first check-up with the doctor to the day of his death, it had been a matter of a few weeks. One minute he was there, the next minute he was gone. Just like that.

As an adult many years later, I had the opportunity to read the nurses' notes that were taken from Brian's bedside. It broke my heart to learn just how fast and how devastating it must have been for my brother to die like that. His whole body was riddled with large growths and a lot of pain. There was continuous bleeding from his nose and mouth. This caused even more suffering; the lack of oxygen left him feeling like he was suffocating to death, and he was. He couldn't eat or sleep and in those days, even though the doctors did their very best, there was little they could do apart from pain control. Finally, late one night the doctor came into Brian's room and gave him his usual pain injection to try and help him out, then he left. Fifteen minutes later the doctor returned and this time he administered the lethal dose of medication needed to end his suffering – and his life. Brian was fifteen. What an act of compassion and courage that must have been. If that doctor is still out there, and someday reads this book, thank you and God bless you.

Although I was only twelve at the time, I can to this day remember a sense of fear and darkness that came over me, a knowing that something had now gone very wrong with our lives. I thought these things only happened on TV or to someone else.

After my dad told us the terrible news, he got up and left the room. I don't think he wanted us kids to see the level of grief and tears he was experiencing. We all looked at each other not knowing what to do. So we just went back to playing on the couch, trying to pretend that nothing had ever happened. But the unfathomable had happened, and as a result something inside our family froze that day. Things would never be the same again.

It wasn't long before the whole neighborhood would hear the news and our doorstep would be covered with flowers, cards and baskets of fruit. Our little world had changed forever. To this day, the smell of roses reminds me of that time; and more specifically everyone's inability to deal with the topic of death. The church service was overflowing with people from all over the area. I can still see my father helping my mother walk slowly down the church steps to the waiting car; the car that took us all to the cemetery where we said our final goodbyes.

Then, as if nothing had ever happened, we never spoke about my brother again. Life just went on, but not without that deep silent wound that comes with the loss of a family member. My family's inability to accept what had happened changed everyone and everything from that moment on.

DEBRIEF

I now have children of my own. I can't imagine what it must have been like for my parents to sit there next to their firstborn child and have to watch him suffer and die in that way.

Buddha said: "All life is illusion and children are the biggest illusion of all." This is why I wanted this story to be the first one told in the second part of this book. It is my earliest memory of suffering and having to come to terms with the loss of someone so close to me.

As an adult, I can see now that life is always giving us the opportunity to let go. It's just that most of us do not see it like that. As a result we learn the hard way, if we ever learn at all. I was young and too inexperienced at the time. I had no idea about the truth of how life works. It is only through a lifetime of hard knocks that I have become friendly with having to let go. Remember, we can only see what our understanding and level of consciousness will allow us to see. It is ignorance of the truth that leads to suffering in life.

I lived for years with a deep hole in my chest from the loss of my brother. I am sure the rest of my family did too. None of us had any idea of how to heal such a deep wound. We were uneducated when it came to the topic of death, yet we were all suddenly confronted with this thing that we feared the most. Fear makes us act in funny ways. The reaction for most of us is to avoid the truth and just hope that it will somehow go away and leave us alone. But it doesn't. It hangs around in the background and haunts us. In fact, it digs deeper into our bodies and emotions and stays there until we have suffered enough to confront our fears about the impermanence of life.

At the time of writing this book, I have spent over thirty years meditating and working on my spiritual development. Although it has helped me in many ways, it still, at times, seems a long way from mastering the art of letting go and living in the moment. Even after my experience of transcending duality in 2005, the writing of this story has brought up a lot of sadness in me. Maybe we never get over it. Maybe this is as good as it gets, even when we can finally accept the way life works.

I mean if you can lose a brother, sister, mother or father and still allow whatever you feel to just be there, without the story you make up about it, you have done a much better job than me on this path. I have learned to let go only through the sheer pain of holding on, when I had no choice, when I was backed into a corner like a cut rattlesnake fighting for its life. Then, and only then, would I cave into reality. The art of letting go is, for most of us, a tough lesson. Only through the relentless agony of our painful experiences do we begin to relinquish our attachments. In the final analysis there is no textbook or bulletproof way of surrendering and allowing things to be the way they are. There are many ways up a mountain and there are just as many ways to develop the skill of letting go. All are valid if it gets you through the night.

Letting go of my brother was a slow process. I don't think my parents ever got over what seemed like a punishment from God. You see, the conceptual mind works in concepts and stories. So when something happens in life, it takes that experience and begins to add its own spin on it. The problem is that we think the story we make up about what happens in life is real. But it is not. It is only the story we invent about what happens to us in life, not the facts.

When this happens, life then becomes what I call a 'real illusion.' When we are not dealing with reality we sooner or later suffer. But when we do deal with reality, there is choice: freedom and power. We mourn the illusions of our life, always ignorant of the truth that lies in front of our very eyes.

In my business life, I often tell the story about the time I was ten and went to my first party. We were in a church basement, with all the boys on one side of the room and all the girls on the other. From what I can recall the boys were terrified of making the first move; we were all pushed up against the wall trying to look cool. My friend kept telling me to go over and ask one of the girls to dance. I finally bucked up the courage and walked across what seemed like the biggest yawning chasm in the universe. As I got to the other side, I looked one of the girls in the eye and asked if she was up for the challenge. Guess what she said? You got it. "No!" The moment she said that, my conceptual mind convinced me it was all because I had big ears, a big nose and skinny legs.

The truth is, she didn't say anything of the sort. But that's what I 'heard' and that experience influenced my behavior well into adulthood. In time, the story I made up about what happened became real and began creating my perception of life when it came to dancing with girls.

So things happen and then we make up a story about why those things happen. This is how the conceptual mind works. When it came to the death of my brother there were some pretty big stories going around. Things like: 'God is punishing us' and 'God always takes the best people first and it should never have happened.' One thing was clear: we were unable to deal with that 'real illusion.' My guess is if we had been able to do that, we may have been able to let go and accept what had happened sooner. My mother swallowed her grief, never spoke of it again and many years later died, I believe, of a broken heart. My father drank away his sorrows and died two years later of the same thing.

So what did I learn from this experience? Well I can see now that no one is exempt when it comes to dying. We are all on the guest list. It happens to millions every day. Looking back, I can see that, from a young age, the universe was teaching me about the power of impermanence. All things are coming and going. The more you can let everything in your life just pass through, the more freedom and peace you experience.

I have gotten better at seeing things for what they are without the story. I can report that there is a lot less suffering when we live in reality and let go of the fantasy of how we want life to be. I mean, I have tried in vain to live out some of my fantasies of fame and glory (see Chapter 8: *Mexico Magic*), but if the truth were told, fantasy is not reality or we would not be calling it a fantasy. But for some crazy reason, most of us are running around thinking our fantasies are real.

In fact, we are so nuts on this planet, we will even kill in the name of fantasy and delusion over the way we perceive things to be. There is no perception or fantasy in reality. Things just are what they are. In fact from a non-dual view, not only are things just what they are, nothing in existence has any real meaning, label or individual identity to it. In the presence of reality there is no story to tell. Why? Because there is no mind to tell a story. No mind, no story.

There is enormous power inherent in being able to distinguish reality from fantasy. It allows us to be with things just as they are, unfiltered and untainted by the conceptual mind. A state commonly known by many as 'enlightenment.'.

CHAPTER 5

Playing Roulette

"When you stop thinking you become a part of everything else that is not thinking."

JC Mac

As you know, the term roulette often refers to a gamble of some type, risking something and taking a chance on life. And that's what this particular story is about: risking and gambling with life; in this case, my life.

There was an area that I grew up in as a young teenager called 'The Valley.' It was a low rental housing development or, what we know in Canada and the U.S. as, *the projects*. It was just a series of government homes all stuck together side by side. Our family moved there because we were financially poor, just like all the other families that lived there. I spent the best part of my teens there. Along with the poverty, there was a lot of addiction and violence and all the other things that take place when you are living at that level of consciousness. I have since learned that heaven has no location; it's a state of consciousness.

This particular level of existence was quite far down the spiritual food chain, so to speak. It was a notorious area where many people eventually ended up in lock-ups, mental institutions, jails, hooked on booze and drugs and even being shot to death. For me, this way of life was normal. We formed gangs and lived committed to each other like the family we never had. Our gang was inseparable, our bonds unbreakable. There was nothing we would not have done for each other. This form of survival included a set of street ethics, all of which helped us to feel safe and part of something special. Bad attention is better than no attention at all.

In fact, because of the things that were going on at home with our parents – all the addiction and dysfunction – most of us spent the majority of our time in the streets together. It was often safer there than it was at home. At least you knew where you stood with your fellow gang members. This was a big part of the reason I ended up spending so much time with these guys.

I was a natural born leader (in a bad kind of way) and would often find myself initiating and planning what we were all going to do for excitement. Much of which, I might add, didn't turn out particularly well. There might have been twenty or thirty of us roaming the streets all night, policing our patch and looking for trouble. If anybody that we didn't know came into our area it was flagged up to the crew as someone trespassing on our turf, and things could turn nasty very quickly. You were entering hallowed ground, uninvited. Not good.

Yet for me, that gang became my family. As crazy as it sounds, the years I spent in that place were some of the most profound and rewarding moments of my life. Our loyalty to each other was unshakeable. I really admired the lengths that we were willing to go for each other. And so this place was where I was to end up spending most of my youth, just hanging around in the streets. Even though a lot of heavy stuff happened in that place, I loved that whole scene. I felt like I fit right in with all the other dysfunctional kids, as I was already messed up long before I got to the projects.

Just like the others, it was a match made in hell. Things were not right mentally, emotionally and spiritually for me and I could sense a big hole right in the middle of my chest, one that I was to spend most of my life trying to fill – with anything I could find. I can now see that spiritual, mental and emotional health is an inside job. But at that time I often walked around with a sense of emptiness, like something was missing and had been from birth. I was always being pursued by a darkness that was deep inside of me and so would do anything not to face it.

And so being in the gang was my compensation for what I didn't get at home. It helped me, to a certain extent, fill that spiritual hole for a while, or at least masked it from the pain of what was missing in my life and what it felt like to be a whole human being. You see, humans always psychologically compensate for what they don't get in their lives. I can also see now that, as far as karma is concerned, what was going on there was necessary as part of my spiritual development. In fact I think that everything we do is part of our development towards the realization that we are all enlightened. It is the illusion of obstacles and our attachment to them that creates all the suffering that blocks our true nature from shining through.

In the evenings the police would often patrol the area trying to keep it safe. But being the crazy bunch of guys that we were, we used the cover of the night to play a game of cat and mouse with them. How this would get started was usually by getting one of the boys to call up the police station and act like an upset neighbor, telling the heat (police) that there were kids making a disturbance in our neighborhood. When they finally arrived to check out what the problem was, we would throw eggs or bricks or anything else we could find at them, and then the chase was on. The whole gang would disperse throughout the projects and, believe me, we knew every little nook and cranny in the area, so getting away was easy.

The police eventually figured out that the best way to get back at us was to target just a couple of us at a time. When they did, the evening's entertainment would begin. The downside was that if you got caught, you usually got a good beating. So it was important to make sure you got away. I actually think the police enjoyed it as much as we did. We not only gave them a run for their money, but it also provided them with something to do on the night shift.

One hot summer night, I was sitting on the curb, just hanging out in the hood, when an unmarked police car pulled up. Two detectives got out, threw me in the back seat and drove off with me. From what I could tell they were interested in getting a bit of payback for some of the things we had done to them. I just happened to be in the wrong place at the right time. So off we went for a drive to some remote area not that far from the projects, one guy behind the wheel and the other monkey in the back seat with me. During the drive the cop in the back seat began asking me questions. Every time I gave him the wrong answer or didn't answer at all, he would pound me in the face with his fists. It didn't take long for things to escalate and eventually he pulled out his thirty-eight revolver and proceeded to pistol-whip me with it. Within seconds I could feel warm blood running from my eyes, nose and down my face.

Then at some point during the ride the cop took the bullets out of his pistol, showed them to me and proceeded to put one round back in the chamber and spin it. He then put the revolver in my mouth and pulled the trigger. Let me tell you, there is nothing like the clicking sound of a trigger from a loaded gun pushed into your head to get you smack-bang into the present moment. The smell of the car, the colors, the sounds and everything that was taking place suddenly became absolutely present for me. It happened all at the same time. There was no sequence of events, just a profound awareness of everything that was occurring, all at once.

This was the game we called roulette, the cost of getting caught for our dirty deeds. I had heard about this game from others. But hearing about it was very different from actually experiencing it for yourself. It is one thing to read the menu at a restaurant and it is another thing to eat the food. It was not for the weak of heart. Even if I could have given them the information they wanted, ratting on my friends was out of the question. Our loyalty to each other far exceeded anything they were ever going to do to me anyway. Funny as it may seem but I still have the problem of being over loyal to this day.

We eventually ended up in some remote location where I was tied to a pole and beaten black and blue. When they were finished my ribs and nose were broken and my eyes were swollen shut. I was then pushed and kicked down an embankment landing next to a set of railway tracks where I stayed for the next hour or so. I eventually got up and made the long journey back through the night to the projects. A friend drove me straight to hospital where I spent the next few days being stitched up and recovering from my wounds. Nothing was ever said or done about it from that moment on. If anything the incident just strengthened my position as someone who was willing to take a beating and still keep his mouth shut.

DEBRIEF

Now here is the crazy thing about all this. When the cop had the gun in my mouth, I knew that I could be facing my final moment, but for some reason there was no fear. I don't know why but I suddenly had a flash of clarity that there was life beyond death. Instantly, I knew that no matter what they did to me, I would live on. In that moment of absolute presence, I could also see that I may not have had any choice about what was happening physically but that ultimately I knew that if I trusted, all would be well.

I felt a sense of immortality and a living connection with all of life. I became one with everything around me. Even the gun in my mouth became part of this reality. It was as if I had faced death many times before – perhaps in past lives, who knows? – and that I had overcome the fear that goes with it. I felt spiritually immortal and bulletproof, if that makes any sense.

As a young boy, I often felt very old inside. It was as if I had some kind of wisdom beyond my years, like I had access to information that other people just didn't have or couldn't see. I don't mean that in an arrogant kind of way. It is just that there were lots of times when things would come out of my mouth that were quite profound. Ancient wisdom, if you like. I can remember once when I was about fourteen, there was a much older friend of mine who was freaking out on drugs. Without any thought about it, I began talking him down, reassuring him that what he was experiencing was a perfectly normal reaction to the drug he was on. I kept telling him that everything was perfect and nothing was out of place. He quickly calmed down and relaxed, and then began laughing at it all. This was a common occurrence for me when my friends were in some kind of crisis. The wisdom would somehow come out of my mouth and speak through me. It felt like it was coming from some place other than my little uneducated mind.

Having the cop put his gun into my mouth was one of those moments. To my astonishment, I completely surrendered to the situation. I looked the cop in the eye and said: "Go ahead, pull the trigger. I dare you." This just pissed him off even more. Probably not the smartest thing to say to a guy with a loaded gun pointed at your head. But that's what came out of my mouth.

In that moment, I realized that there is a choice when one is faced with the possibility of death. That choice is either to let go and trust, or to hold on in fear and limitation. Like I said earlier, I can't prove any of this but my instincts keep telling me that the decision you make at that moment has a lot to do with influencing what happens next. Your intentions and decisions have a huge impact on the field of consciousness. Everything in existence is influencing everything else in existence. Now, there's a tough one to swallow.

Things get very interesting when you are faced with what seems to be your last breath. Living through that changes you. It leaves you with a different view of life, a very powerful view of life. Every fear we manage to overcome in life sets us free. Everything we confront contributes to whom we become as spiritual beings undergoing a human experience.

A good example of this is when I started taking my two sons, Matt and James, to the skateboard park. As much as they wanted to go down the big ramp, I could see the fear preventing them from doing it. I worked with them week after week, educating them around how fear holds us back in life and that each time you overcome what frightens you, it makes you a stronger, more confident and capable person. Fear can be used as a healthy illusion only when one has transcended it.

I continued to inch them closer and closer to the edge until, suddenly, one day I watched their fear turn into trust and courage. It was at that moment they both took the plunge down the steep ramp. The transformation on their little faces was spectacular and a joy to see. They have never been the same since. From then on, they truly owned the skateboard park.

This is what I mean when I say prepare yourself for death. Learn the nature of reality. Walk into the fire so that you too will be able to take the plunge and transform fear into trust. There is nothing I can think of that is more important than this. The path is narrow. There is little time, so learn how to die like a warrior. This for me is true freedom in life.

CHAPTER 6

The Green Shelby

"The less you think, the more peace you experience."
JC Mac

Steve was a friend of mine that I used to hang around with in the projects. He was one of those guys who really loved working on cars, or, as we used to call them in those days, grease monkeys. I was never really much into that scene, but Steve loved it. Every one of my monkey friends drove around either in some kind of old jacked up Ford, Chevy or on a Harley Davidson bike.

I don't know how he ever got his hands on it, but one day Steve showed up with this beautiful green Shelby Mustang GT500. And like all the other car nuts in those days, he immediately went to work on ripping it apart and finding ways to make it move and handle even faster than it already could – not that it needed it. This was the kind of car that would be banned if ever seen on the roads today. But back then there were no restrictions on what you could do to improve on the speed and maneuverability of a monster like the Shelby.

The name of the game was to get every inch of power out of that baby without killing yourself in the process. No seatbelts, no nothing in those days. Just one big hell of a motor, four on the floor and a good looking body. And oh let's not forget the leather backed seats…(ya baby that's what I'm talkin' about).

Back then it was common for people to drive over the legal alcohol limit. In fact, in the projects one of the silly little lines was: 'If you can't walk, drive.' And sooner or later that's exactly what would happen. We would become so hammered from drinking and taking drugs that the only way left to get around was to drive. Ouch.

So one evening, after a heavy session of partying, we decided to take the green devil out for a spin. That was our first mistake as we were both well over the drink/drive legal limit at the time. Let me repeat that: We were well over the limit – I mean *really* over the limit.

So being the crazy guys that we were it made perfect sense to get into the Shelby and take off. Within seconds we were tearing down the street, music blasting out of the windows (eight track cassettes in those days), a trail of white and blue smoke behind us, heading towards the city lights. As Steve continued to push the pedal to the metal, we suddenly heard that all too familiar sound of a police siren and noticed its flashing lights illuminating the city streets. The first thing that came over me was a deep fear, as we both knew that big trouble was on the way. If caught, the Shelby would certainly be impounded and we would be headed for another tour of duty in the local jail. Not good.

At first, Steve slowed down and pulled over to the curb and the police car proceeded to do the same thing right behind us. The officer got out and started walking towards the Shelby. Then Steve suddenly changed his mind. "Ah, the hell with it," he said and hammered his foot down on the gas. We screeched off in a cloud of smoke, leaving the smell of burning rubber behind us. What a sight (and sound) to behold. The chase was on.

Being in the passenger seat, there wasn't really anything I could do other than begin to throw the drugs and remaining alcohol out the window (what a waste that was.) I certainly wasn't about to open the door and jump out. I could see the policeman in the rear-view mirror frantically running through the cloud of white smoke and back to his car. The one thing I did know was that the police car was never going to match the speed of that Shelby. It was just too fast. That was the good news. The bad news was that his car had a radio and it didn't take long before there were another five cars on our tail. The police also began radioing our co-ordinates ahead and blocking off all the intersections along our route.

It was about three o'clock in the morning and the streets were empty. We stood out like a sore thumb, not to mention the sound of

THE ANATOMY OF A SPIRITUAL MELTDOWN

that Shelby's roaring engine and the police sirens behind us. Steve picked up more and more speed. I could see he had no intention of stopping or being pinched. By this point there was no turning back; we were already in too deep. The only thing we could do now was to try and get away, but I think we both knew the chances of that were getting slimmer and slimmer as we continued speeding down the city streets, with the blur of white lines and houses flashing by.

Steve just kept accelerating and looking for a way out. Let me tell you, doing 140 miles an hour through city streets is a terrifying experience, especially with police hot on your tail. The thought of what they would do to us when they did manage to block us in… Well, let's just say my head was not yet ready to go there.

Then, suddenly, through a minefield of internal terror, I had a realization. It dawned on me that I was utterly powerless and there was absolutely nothing I could do except go along for the ride. Whatever was going to happen was going to happen. As we continued to barrel down the road I began to let go into the fear and the danger of the situation, and as I did, I started to relax. Then suddenly, I became aware that all thought in my head had disappeared, leaving me present to everything that was happening.

I could smell the rubber from the wheels, the leather from the seats and the warm summer night air blowing in through the windows. I could hear every nuance of sound pumping out of the car engine and the stereo. It felt like being a very talented conductor who can hear each individual instrument simultaneously. I could witness and experience everything that was happening, all at the same time, moment to moment.

Everything around me began to light up and become stunningly beautiful. All movement started to slow down, and as it did I became overwhelmed by a silent, still peacefulness. The world of form and all its distractions had faded into the background. I just 'knew' that I was going to be alright, that death once again was not a possibility in reality. So I just surrendered and let go into the experience. I sat there in the passenger seat until, eventually, the police had blocked off the streets and we had nowhere left to go. The party was over.

    We were dragged out of the car, beaten, arrested and thrown in jail. It was on the ride to the police station that I began to notice that my thinking had returned and life was back to the ego-based world of separation and survival. That beautiful moment of divinity in the presence of the way things truly are was obscured once again by the mind.

DEBRIEF

This is not a long story but, for me, it is a very profound one. It points once again to what happens when the mind stops – and what it takes to make it stop. I've met many people who have had similar experiences during traumatic events that left them in the stunning presence of reality – and you can only truly experience this when all thought vanishes unannounced. They may not have recognized it as such, but at that moment one is catapulted into the presence of the way things really are and that is one hell of a sight to see. When one stops thinking reality appears, just as when thinking arises reality disappears. That's a profound distinction. When you are present, divinity is present and that can only take place without thought. That's really the long and short of it.

So how does one make their mind stop without having to go through a life threatening experience? Well, one thing I do know is that you cannot think your way into not thinking. There is no formula or ten easy steps to enlightenment, because that would require a mind, the very thing that is in the way to begin with. Part of the answer, I believe, comes from a simple lack of education on the true nature of reality and how the mind works. I mean, we don't send our kids to school and for the first half hour each morning have them sitting cross-legged, breathing calmly and meditating so that they can begin to experience the silence of divinity. No. What we do is continually keep engaging their minds to think; to do instead of to be. When we break it down we can see, first and foremost, that all doing comes from 'being.' Not the other way round. But the dilemma arises yet again, as we cannot 'do' being.

Can you imagine what it would be like just to *be*, instead of always just do – and what that would make available to someone's life? To your life? For the most part we just stumble along, trying to find peace and happiness by consuming things outside of ourselves, hoping it will give us what we need. We are unconsciously addicted to using our minds as a tool for doing, and doing just leads to more doing. True happiness is the art of being.

When my son was only eight years old he asked me: "Is God a person?" So even at that age he is trying to conceptualize divinity through duality. All of this arises out of a lack of understanding of the true nature of reality. Remember, duality is just an illusion of the ego looking outside itself at the world and interpreting what it thinks it sees. The ego operates at a level of consciousness that obscures the view of one's true nature. Duality is a real illusion.

The truth can often appear when one is confronted with their own mortality. Because of the shock that comes with the thought of suddenly not existing, one becomes present like they have never been before. What we call the conceptual mind is not interested in the present moment. The reason for this is because it can't exist there. It's not designed to be present. It functions by projection, into either the so-called past or the so-called future, always creating some kind of drama as a way of avoiding the truth, so that it can keep itself in a position of thinking it is running the show.

To be completely in the present moment, one would have to stop thinking and the ego cannot work without thought. Your current inner conversation is being shaped and formed out of your current level of consciousness, one that often includes the illusion of ego.

Our perception of life is not only produced by our predominant level of consciousness, but is also influenced by the conditioning of our upbringing; what you absorbed from your parents, school and the culture around you. All this contributes to your perception and how you view the world; or the story you have built up about how you view the world. It all works like a set of filters that tint your view of reality. That to the ego is heavenly juice to feed off. It keeps it alive, and the job of the ego is to survive life at any cost. The ego is so stupid it will even throw you off a bridge before it will surrender its position of thinking it's the boss (go figga).

Now I am not saying the ego is a bad thing. It has been very helpful in the development of humanity and all that we have created.

But when it comes to emerging into a state of divinity, it is our biggest stumbling block. It will even tell you that it wants to become an enlightened ego, but in reality that is not a possibility. Like I have said, the ego has a workable function in life, but first it needs to know its place, and that place is to serve and not to rule.

Remember, as long as there is perception there is illusion. Beyond the mind there is no perception, simply because there is no ego anymore. It is the ego that creates the illusion of perception. The internal conversation you are having is being manufactured out of the ego and the ego, as I have said, exists only at a given level of consciousness. When one reaches a high enough level of consciousness (there are no levels in reality), the illusion of the ego vanishes and when that happens one's internal conversation goes with it.

One could look at consciousness as a high-speed internet connection with many different bandwidths, and at each bandwidth you have access to all the information in that bandwidth. The level profoundly influences how we see and what we think, and, ultimately, it determines behavior.

Being in the present moment is a difficult task for any prolonged length of time. I am sure many seasoned mediators will agree with me on that one. The busier the mind the more one suffers. If you look closely you can see this suffering playing out in people everywhere. You can see just what the mind is capable of putting them through, even if they are not aware of it. It shows up in their faces, the tensions in their bodies and lives, the way they walk and breathe. All of these are affected by the incisive nature of the mind.

The ego loves the suffering it inflicts on the mind because it keeps it alive and in control. This process can have a very detrimental effect on one's mental, emotional and physical wellbeing. It shoots itself in the foot by burning itself out because of its own ignorance of the truth. It just doesn't know that its salvation is in the present moment; and that it can still exist but in a different way, a much more productive and peaceful way. But that requires it to become like an employee instead of the company owner. Sadly, that is out of the question for most ego-driven people. Especially people like me…

I recently spent time with a friend of mine who was dying. I told her: "If you don't know how to die, you don't know how to live." She had a hard time understanding what I meant by this. I said: "Well, when you know the next moment is going to be your last, you'll appreciate the current one." And we're not very good at that. We don't use the reality of dying to our advantage. An encounter with death can be a great clarifier and a way of getting people present very quickly (in reality there is no such thing as a moment or becoming present, but I have no other language to describe what I am trying to say).

To be completely present means the death of the ego and that's really the only death worth mastering. We live like we are never going to die, like it's going to go on forever, so we don't bother with what is available in this moment. But somewhere underneath that, in a low grade energy field, what we're really doing is trying to arrange life so that death doesn't come knocking, so that it passes us by. We avoid having any kind of bad health, taking too much risk, losing our possessions in life or all our money. We look for ways to play it safe and avoid danger. We arrange our life to become more and more risk averse, all in a vain attempt to try to sneak by the inevitable taking place. This is insane – and it means we're missing what's going on right now. If you're not present to what's happening right now then you are missing out on your life. The ego is great at having us miss everything that is important for living a full and peaceful life. We seek, and we seek, and we seek, but we never really find. True peace only comes when one stops thinking and seeking altogether.

Many of us are not aware of the benefits of being in the present moment, simply because we have never experienced it. What most of us consider the present moment is actually more about wandering around in concepts of the past and the future, but certainly not in the present. And we settle for that because we have been doing it for so long it seems utterly normal to us. We are like trained rats; all you have to do is ring the bell and we will react. We think that the smarter we become, the more we engage with life, but in fact, it's the opposite. The more you think, the further away you are from reality and your true nature. You cannot think your way to heaven.

I know I keep repeating this and here it is again. One cannot be present to reality while thought is going on. Thought filters your reality – how things really are and how life really works. It is an insidious white noise that continues to run in the background all the time. It is similar to living near an airport. After a while, you no longer notice the planes flying overhead. When the mind is in operation, we become trapped in the illusion of thought and what appears to be reality.

So learning the art of being present by beginning to consider the fact that the next moment could be your last moment is a powerful practice. You can really start to be here and enjoy what's going on moment to moment when you're not thinking. Life becomes a real joy. You start enjoying the full living color of all its beauty.

If the truth were told, any of us could drop dead in the next moment, in the middle of our next phone call, or while walking to the shops. So how do we learn to be present and extract every drop of joy out of every moment we are alive? Tough job. For most of us, almost impossible.

No self-help book or course can give you the formula to this kind of living. If they did, most of us would have found it years ago. When someone tells you they have the answer to life, run a mile. There are many ways up a mountain. The path to heaven for most of us begins in hell. This certainly has been true in my case. For most it is the steepest rock face they will ever decide to climb. I have stumbled through and made every possible mistake you can in search of the truth – often doing more damage than good, both to myself and to others around me.

My belief these days in terms of the fast track to enlightenment is summed up in this little statement: 'Screw everything up all the time.' Then, when there's been enough suffering and the illusion has been shattered, the divine light of reality will spontaneously shine forth. No guts, no glory. It takes courage and true leadership to be willing to confront the final door.

Through being up close and personal many times with the possibility of losing my life, I have realized that what is truly important is this moment. I mean if I wanted to learn any other skill I would practice it. So it makes sense to practice being in this moment as a way of living in peace.

Think of the comfort and the certainty that would come to your life if you could experience that level of letting go, if you could surrender to the unknown with total trust. It is like walking the high wire at the circus without a net. If you could have that experience now – and it is possible – then there is no fear of life, as fear is no more than a projection of what we think is coming or not coming in the next moment. When accomplished we have serenity in the midst of the storm. It is only then that you really start to enjoy life because you're not concerned about the outcome anymore. One is here now, moment to moment.

CHAPTER 7

Home On The Range

"Heaven has no location but is a state of no mind."
JC Mac

This story is about how conditions, when appropriate, can lead to an experience of 'no mind'; a state of having no thought, conceptual or otherwise. The Chinese Zen master Huang Po, who lived over a thousand years ago, said that the pathway to enlightenment is by cutting through the mind and all the concepts that give meaning to our lives. In essence, it is about dissolving the stories we have about what we think is real. When you can do this, what emerges is a view of things just the way they are, without interpretation, names or labels. From this perspective, everything looks stunning. There are no more filters.

As I said earlier, when I was young I grew up in a rough and poor neighborhood. Even though there were tough times, I really didn't mind, as the street was always full of guys hanging out all night. In fact, for me, there was something magical about those hot summer nights in the projects. The city heat would bake down on us as we all wandered the streets looking for trouble. We would do anything to take away the boredom of our young lives.

To this day, I often think of the love and sense of camaraderie we had together. For us, it was safer hanging out on the streets with our friends than it was at home. We all helped, protected and watched over each other. Anyone who wandered into our neighborhood by mistake ran the risk of being beaten by the gang. It took very little to start a fight on our patch. In fact we all looked forward to it.

'The Valley' was our little corner of the world, and with that you took on all the trouble and risk that came with it. Most of us were out there on the streets because of broken families, poverty, crime, drugs and too much alcohol, all of which is common at that level of consciousness.

I often ended up in a lot of trouble simply because everyone else was ending up that way and it was a game of follow the leader. Looking back, I now see that everyone is a leader in life. It's just a question of whether we are any good at it. This place was full of bad leadership and a total lack of responsibility. As we began to grow up, some of the guys managed to get themselves through school, moved out and forged new lives elsewhere. But not me. I loved it there and never wanted to leave.

Strange as it might sound, The Valley was my spiritual home, my training ground. It was all I had, so I think that was why I stayed for so long. I felt empty inside due to a lack of parenting in our family. I mean, I loved and respected my parents and the job they tried to do with us, but it takes a lot more than love to have your life turn out. It takes good communication, skill, leadership and setting the right example; and there was very little of that going on in our hood.

So the gang got smaller and as it did the guys who stayed started getting into more and more serious trouble. What started out as petty crime evolved into violent crime and people started getting hurt. Some even killed. A lot of the guys went off into bike gangs where guns, violence and drugs became part of the scene. As it got more dangerous, it got more difficult to break free. That's what was so hard, because there was a loyalty that kept us bound to each other, no matter what.

Finally in my late teens I realized that I needed to break away from the gang or I'd end up in prison, crazy or dead. One definition of insanity is doing the same thing over and over again but expecting a different result. I knew I had to do something different if I was going to have any kind of a life at all.

I got thinking about ways that I could move up and improve on my life. As I did I began to remember my early years as a young boy when I had spent time in Tacoma, Washington, with my Uncle

THE ANATOMY OF A SPIRITUAL MELTDOWN

Pete who was a U.S. fighter pilot, and how much respect I had for what he did in life. He was the first real leader I had ever met. He later volunteered for service in Vietnam and never came home. But that's another story.

So I thought that maybe the military would help me learn to make something of my life. With my uncle, I had experienced what it was like to be around integrity and honor and I could see the power in that way of living. That kind of thing was unheard of in my neighborhood.

So like a good little soldier boy I decided to join the army, and when I did, off to boot camp I went. As funny as it may sound, I really did like the discipline and the military way of life. In fact, I began to thrive on it, just like I had in The Valley. It was there, during my training as a soldier, that this story really begins, out there on the firing line while learning the art of killing. The perfect job for a screwed up street kid, don't you think?

We used to practice this art daily. Our platoon of about twenty-five young men were all itching to get busy and checked out (qualified) on all the weapons. There would be crates and crates of ammunition laid out all over the range. We would spend hours upon hours out in the field honing our skills, until finally the sergeant would give the order to pack up and head back to the barracks. There was a strict rule that no live rounds were ever to be taken from or left on the range. Crazy as it sounds, there were often guys trying to mail home bullets and live rounds as souvenirs to their friends and family. No one was ever allowed to leave the range until all the live ammo had been spent and everyone had been checked over in case they were trying to sneak some of it away.

One hot summer's day, as we were finishing a day of mayhem at the office, my sergeant called a halt to all the firing. He then organized the team to head back to the barracks and as he did he also ordered me to stay behind and finish off the remaining ammo. So there I was on my own, left with the task of dispensing of all the open crates of munitions in whatever way I saw fit. What an opportunity! My primal dream of being able to just cut loose and create as much damage and noise as possible had just come true.

In what seemed to feel like forever I started loading all the clips and magazines. There were thousands of rounds and all types of weapons to play with. The other point worth mentioning here is that, as a result of my upbringing, I had become a very angry young man and this was part of my reason for joining the military. I mean what better place to vent your unresolved issues in life than in combat or weapons training? This was going to be the cheapest therapy on the market. Don't try this at home kids.

I could feel the hot August sun beating down on me as I began to cut loose with all this firepower at my fingertips. Blue smoke and the sound of gunfire filled the air and with it came this feeling of relief from years of pent up anger and frustration. Within moments things began to escalate to an insane pace. The orange glow of the sun disappeared behind the smoke from the machine guns, handguns, automatic rifles and grenades.

Then suddenly, as the last round was fired, everything went quiet. The smoke slowly lifted from all that chaos and gently disappeared up into the summer sky. As it did, I began to notice that everything around me had gone into slow motion and was completely silent, once again. The next thing I realized was that all thinking had vanished and I could no longer find the voice in my head. There was only a still silent awareness of all of life and its stunning beauty. I was left in a state of profound, absolute bliss. I couldn't move and so just stood there paralyzed as an infinite field of still, loving silence rocketed me into another dimension.

After some time – I am not sure how long – that tormenting inner voice of mine returned and with it came my identity. As the voice started up again the world reappeared as a kind of black and white movie. Remember the scene in 'The Wizard of Oz' when it goes from black and white to color? Well, it was like that in reverse. It suddenly struck me just how powerful the conversation in my head was and how it blocks out the light of God.

With the stunning beauty of divinity gone, I was back to my old self, standing on the firing range with an empty weapon in my hands. The paradigm shift from the linear to the non-linear and back again, left me shocked and bewildered. I finally packed up my kit and returned to the barracks, never to mention my experience to anyone, until the writing of this book many years later.

DEBRIEF

When there is no thought, there is no filter between you and reality. If you think life can look beautiful when you're thinking about it, you should see what's there when you are not thinking about it. It is like God turning up the color and beauty volume of all things. Everything begins to radiate a living field of profound still silence that I can only describe as the love of divinity. Not only do you begin to see yourself in everything but everything sees itself in you.

The funny (or not so funny) thing about having no voice inside your head is that when it goes, so does your identity. This can be very unnerving in the beginning, as we have lived our lives relating to this voice in our head, and what it tells us about who were are – and who we think we are not. Without a voice there is no conversation about your past or future– it is no longer relevant as you become aware that both of those ideas are just concepts and a projection of the conceptual mind. No voice equals no concept and no concept equals no identity, because identity is a concept – if you know what I mean.

The experience of everything going completely silent and still was so overwhelming, I couldn't actually move. I just stood there, stunned at the profound beauty of it all. At first it was an awareness of reality without thought, followed by the sudden realization that I was reality, which, by the way, is me yet again contradicting myself, as the word 'I' insinuates duality. Because if there is an 'I' then there is a 'you,' which means we are trapped yet again. Sorry about that. I am trying to explain a non-dual state with the faulty tool of words. Words are form and form is duality. (Believe me I am more frustrated than you are about trying to get these points and insights across.) Oh the hell with it, lets just get back to the debrief, OK?

For the third time in my life, I felt that I was one with all things, that there was no longer any separation between me and everything else. It was like coming home after being lost for many lifetimes of suffering and struggle. It reminded me of that childhood

THE ANATOMY OF A SPIRITUAL MELTDOWN

feeling when your mom tucks you into bed and tells you she loves you and everything is going to be alright.

The tough thing about all of this is just how difficult it can be to get as much as a glimpse of this still sense of no mind. There is no quick fix or silver bullet that will guarantee this outcome. I wanted to call this story 'Home on the Range' because the experience felt like I had come home from a long journey away from my own life. It was to be many, many years before I got to experience that kind of peace again. When the world of duality returned so did everything that goes with it. I was back with that familiar old sense of separation; the overriding feeling that it was me against the world. I was back at my job of trying to look good and survive life.

Remember, the less thinking you do, the more peace you experience. When you stop thinking you become part of everything else in the universe that is not thinking. It is our thinking mind and ego that tricks us into perceiving we are separate from everything else in life. The sense of a me and a you, an up and a down, light and dark – even right and wrong – vanishes in the presence of no-mind.

The ego would rather stay separate than see life together as one. It is not designed for unity but instead was developed over time for the purpose of survival. It is only really interested in getting what it wants and perpetuating its own existence. But it can't do that if it sees everything as part of the same thing – because there is nothing to compete with anymore, nothing to go after or survive. There is no hierarchy of importance in life because all things radiate the same beauty, no matter what they are. The timeline and sequential illusion of life and separation completes itself.

In that brief moment of bliss out there on the range, everything seemed alive; the trees, the grass, the sky. I know this is hard to believe, but even the weapons on the range and all the destruction I had managed to create looked just as beautiful as everything else. All of existence is like an intelligent living magnetic field of communication. So, when you transcend duality, you see that everything is alive and giving off its own vibration, based on its so-called level of consciousness.

From this perspective everything can be used as our teacher; everything that happens can be used to our spiritual advantage when we are willing to see it that way. But one must first become aware of how the game of life works to even attempt to practice this kind of living and dying. Yes there are many roads to redemption but none in my experience is as peaceful.

CHAPTER 8

Mexico Magic

"Miracles are normal operating procedure for God, on the battlefield of human life."

JC Mac

When I was twelve years old, I found a guitar in a rubbish bin while walking home from school one day. I couldn't believe my luck. Someone had painted the whole thing white with what looked like house paint. That was just not cool enough for me, so I took it home and sanded it down until all you could see was the natural wood finish. Wow! I was in heaven. I had always loved music, but our family didn't have the money to pay for music lessons, nor could I play any kind of instrument. For me this had been some kind of sign from the heavens that this was my destiny (there goes the conceptual mind once again). I imagined that the great Greek god Zeus (or whichever one of those guys was responsible for having my life turn out) had seen my potential and was sending me on a mission: My job now was to change the world through a series of blistering guitar solos and massive fame. (I think not.)

I spent years just sitting in my room banging away, listening to vinyl records and trying to make it sound like I knew what I was doing. I can still hear my dad yelling up the stairs at me to shut that racket up or he was going to use the guitar that I had in my hands for firewood. From that point on I made sure my practice times took place during his work hours or when he was out doing other things.

I eventually got pretty good at it and began playing in local bands. We would travel around, performing in church basements, or just any old place that would let us set up. Once in a while people would even show up. I can't tell you how many gigs we played to empty venues, but that never really bothered me. I was just happy to be up there doing my thing.

I can remember one gig in a country and western bar, called 'The Winchester,' of all names. It was smack-bang in the middle of the worst part of town. In fact if you managed to get to the gig without some kind of confrontation, it was a bloody miracle. If your car still had wheels on it when you came out of the bar, it was an even bigger miracle.

Then there was the perilous job of setting up your equipment in front of a bunch of drunken cowboys who couldn't wait to take a round out of you, no matter how good your cover tunes set list was. And, trust me, ours was not very good at all. In fact, it was brutal. I should really have listened in school or prayed to a different deity for help. It began to look as if Zeus was about to let me down.

As I got into my teens I really began to improve, and as I did I also noticed that the parties that went with the music started to become even more important than the music. So now, instead of spending the time to really hone my craft, I was indulging more and more in women, drugs, booze and the whole rock and roll lifestyle.

I was part of the hippie movement in the late sixties and seventies, the whole scene in San Francisco and the 'tune in, turn on and drop out' atmosphere of the concerts in Golden Gate Park. The park often put on these free concerts and, when they did, our band would head out early so we could get a spot as close to the stage as possible. We saw some great artists, people like Carlos Santana, The Doors, Janis Joplin, Jefferson Airplane and many others of that time. I loved it but the inspiring influence they had on me was not to last.

I can remember to this day the moment that the partying took over the music. It was the turning point and marked the beginning of the end of that career for me. Later in life, I was to really regret this. I knew I had talent but, in spite of that, I still managed to throw it all away.

You see, in my neighborhood and for most of us there were only a couple of ways out. One was sport and the other was music. Yes, there was the educational route but it was tough for the guys in the hood to discipline themselves to finish school. There wasn't the motivation and support at home that would allow us to study properly and as a result most of us were left to figure life out on our own.

So my music career just slowly tanked and slipped away. That burning desire I had started out with had now shifted and became a hobby that I picked up once in a while, and as life went on, so did the parties. Meanwhile, the so-called normal people (and I have come to see that, these days, 'normal' is only a setting on the household dryer) were out there building careers and families.

But for me, I kept trying to relive the good old days. I just never wanted to leave that time behind, and as a result remained stuck in a fantasy for many years. I had gotten hooked on getting high all the time and, predictably, this eventually began to destroy my life, like it had for so many others that I knew. Then through a series of what I used to call bad breaks and misunderstandings (yeah, right) I ended up in front of a court judge who sentenced me to a young offenders program that was to change the course of my life.

I spent the next few years working out the reasons for my self-destructive behavior until I finally came to terms with things and managed to attain a little peace of mind. As I took stock of my life, I realized how much I missed the music that had inspired me so much as a young man – and that there was unfinished business to take care of. So I bought myself an old beat up guitar once again and started writing songs and getting myself back into musical shape.

The spirit of music had returned. There was nothing like the feeling of getting it right note for note; the sounds that would come out when you suddenly would hit the zone, when everything just flowed without effort. But it wasn't paying the bills, so I had to go out and get a job to support my passion. I was living in Vancouver at this point and got myself a position as a drug and alcohol counselor. I mean, why not? I had managed to become an expert on the topic while partying myself almost to death. My expertise on how to mess up a good thing was now turning into an advantage to serve others. Isn't it funny how God works?

Also, working with people has always come very naturally to me. As a young boy, I realized I was a pretty good communicator. I seemed to have access to some old wisdom that would just pop out whenever it was needed. I never knew where it came from. It was just there – and still is. The only difference now is that I have had many years' experience of working with it. Like a sixth sense of knowing.

So there I was sitting in my room writing all these songs and making my way in the world as a drugs and alcohol counselor. I worked in the local penitentiary, designing recovery and street programs for people trying to integrate back into society. I spent a few years working in detox and treatment centers and then finally became responsible for running the in-house recovery programs at a set of halfway houses for men. Altogether, there were beds for up to around seventy-five guys, all of whom were pretty hardcore. Our clients included every kind of criminal, addict and alcoholic you could possibly think of.

During that time I managed to hear just about everything that one desperate human being can do to another – I mean I really heard some nasty stuff. One day over lunch, an ex-con I was working with calmly mentioned to me in passing that he had stabbed a guy four times. Upon questioning him why he did such a thing, he simply replied that the guy deserved it. Then he asked me to pass the salt. Alrighty then, I thought to myself.

Working with people at that level of existence can be very draining. People like that don't have much to give, as they are generally too unwell to think of anyone but themselves. You can't give what you don't have and so I kept giving and they kept on taking.

Many would call up with all kinds of excuses, trying to get themselves into our program. Some just wanted to be able to impress the judge at their pending court case. Others would say they needed to save the job they never really had. The phone rang all day long with people looking for beds, but most guys never really had any intention of cleaning up. I used to tell the incoming callers that I only had one bed left (even if there were twenty left) and unless they gave me the right answer as to why I should give it to them, they never made it in. Once someone was lucky enough to get through the door, I would sit them down and say to them: "We will do whatever we can to support your integration back into society. But, if for any reason, you make the fatal error of mistaking kindness for weakness with us, then you're out." The criminal mind thinks that if you are kind and nice it means you're being weak. And being weak means that you should be taken for everything you've got. And believe me, these guys were experts at doing that.

In between writing songs in my spare time and working at the halfway house, two years passed. But the longer I worked at the center , the more burned out I became. Every day I was running group therapy, counseling and listening to everyone's problems. But that is the kind of work you can only do for so long before it begins to affect your own peace of mind, and you run the risk of becoming sick yourself. Ultimately, that is exactly what happened. I became a casualty of my own success and burned out. There was nothing left for me to give. I had to leave that job to take care of my own spiritual wellbeing.

The music wasn't making me any money and going back into rehab work would have killed me. So I decided to take a holiday. I didn't own much at the time, but what I did have I just gave away and bought myself a plane ticket to Mexico. I never really had a plan (not like I ever did), I just thought I would head out and see where life took me. At the very least there would be a beach and a little sunshine. So I packed up and headed for the sun.

I ended up in a little place called Puerto Vallarta that, on reflection, had its wonderful moments, but I needed some time alone just to chill and recover from all the darkness I had been exposed to. A local guy agreed to take me to a remote little place that was only accessible by boat. The ride out there was beautiful. We glided through the clear, blue sea under the Mexican sun with dolphins jumping out of the water alongside us. I breathed in the salty sea air and thought: 'Oh yeah. This is going to be a great place to rejuvenate.'

So, I got myself settled into this little village, found myself a small hut with a hammock and just started to chill out. I would walk into town every day to get fresh bread and supplies. I loved it. Just wandering through the beauty of the jungle, slowly letting go of all the darkness that was stuck to me from working with such emotionally sick people.

Slowly, and day by day, I began to move towards the light again. At times during this process I would have nightmares about the things I had heard and experienced. The stories of some of the terrible things these men had done to other people were coming back. I realized it would take a little while to clean up my psyche and get it all out of my system. So I decided to move even deeper into the jungle, to completely isolate myself from the human race. I just couldn't be around people. It was like I had become tainted by humanity, and all it was capable of doing to each other.

So, I packed up my bag and off I went into the wilderness. I just began walking deeper and deeper up the jungle path until I stumbled onto an old hut that was tucked up against the dense hills. It was habitable, close enough to town if I needed anything and remote enough to be away from people. And, believe it or not, there was a beat up old guitar sitting there in the corner. I thought it was magic. A perfect place to recover and tend to my spiritual wounds. I spent most of my time just sitting there, banging away on the guitar and working on my songs. It was great therapy for me. It was how I managed to let go of many of those dark experiences I had encountered back in Vancouver.

Then one sunny day, while I was strumming away on the guitar, this guy came walking out of the jungle and headed towards the hut. This was very unusual given how far away I was from civilization. My first thought was, what the hell is he doing all the way out here – he must be as nuts as me? He then began to make his way over and we began chatting.

I told him how I had ended up there and that I was working on my music. "Oh, let's hear some of it then," he said. I was embarrassed but he insisted. When I finally finished playing him a few songs, he said: "That's good stuff. What are you doing with it?" I told him that, ever since I was young, it had always been a dream of mine to record an album. "So," he said, "what is stopping you?"

"Money, as usual."

"How much money?"

"Oh, nothing that 20,000 dollars wouldn't clear up."

Now here's where the miracle comes in. The next thing that came out of his mouth was: "I'll give you the twenty grand to make your album."

Now I have to say at this point, that although I was born at night, it wasn't *last* night. So my first thought was that he had obviously been in the jungle far too long, eating too many mushrooms with the Incas or something. My next thoughts were: 'Take me to your people!' And: 'What color is the sky in your world.'

"No, really," he reassured me, "I'm serious. Here, write down my details and call me when you get back." And off he disappeared again into the jungle, just as mysteriously as he had arrived.

I stuck his details in my bag and, for the next month, just concentrated on getting well.

When I finally got back home, I couldn't get the words "I'll give you twenty grand" out of my mind. Was this guy for real? Or was he just some whacko who was living out his deluded fantasies at my expense? I finally thought 'what the hell' and dialed his number. When he answered the phone I was shocked into silence. I finally managed to introduce myself. He then asked me if I was still working on the album and did I still wanted the money to produce it. I paused again. Then I thought to myself: 'just go along with it – what the hell do you have to lose?' So the next words out of my mouth were: "Yes that would be great."

"Give me your bank details," he said, "and you will have the money in your account within the next week." I never heard from him again. But, true to his word, within a week there was 20,000 US dollars in my account. So off I went to make the album of my dreams.

DEBRIEF

Though I wasn't that aware of it at the time, part of the reason I wanted to be a famous musician was to prove to everyone that I was someone, that I could succeed, that I was worthy of their attention. I thought that if I could just show my parents, my friends and all the people that I had grown up with in the projects that I was 'good enough,' I would be loved and adored. (Wrong again.) There was a lifetime of people to whom I wanted to be able to say: "See? I told you so. I told you I'd make it." And music was going to be my way of doing that.

This need for attention and success was part of the driving force that had me practice so hard. Yet this was not really the healthiest way to become a good musician – or a good anything – because it was driven out of a dysfunction, or one might say a compensation for what I was never given as a child. Remember, any attention, whether it is good or bad, is better than no attention at all. Looking back I can see that what I was learning was that there is no such thing as freedom when you're doing things out of a compensation.

During the making of my album there was a moment when I was alone in the studio. Everyone had gone out for lunch and I was supposed to be laying down some final vocal tracks. Standing inside this huge vocal booth alone, it suddenly occurred to me that I had done it. I had accomplished my dream and finished the recording of my music. The only thing was, all the people that I had wanted to impress with my artistic creation had all gone from my life. There was no one around for me to say: "See. I told you so. I am worthy now." I suddenly felt a sense of loneliness and depression as it dawned on me just how much of my life I had spent on this project – for all the wrong reasons.

When you suffer from low self-worth like I did at the time, you go out into the world seeking all kind of things to try and fill the hole in your heart, just so you can feel that you are 'enough.' But the emptiness remains and cannot be filled by any person, place or thing

THE ANATOMY OF A SPIRITUAL MELTDOWN

outside one's self. Now try to remember that I am always switching back and forth from a linear to a non-linear conversation, as words cannot explain the unexplainable. In a non-dual world, one that is beyond the illusion of separation, none of this so-called outside stuff like approval or admiration exists. Separation, as I have mentioned, is a function of the ego and beyond duality the ego vanishes. But one doesn't really get to see that until they are at a particular level of consciousness. Under the illusion of duality one always ends up with exactly what they think they are worth in life. You might say that, in life, we get exactly what we are willing to tolerate, and I had managed to develop toleration down to a fine art.

Hollywood and the music industry are full of people that are compensating for what they did not get as a kid; people who think that once they reach the top of their game, their life will turn out. But as we have seen life demonstrate time and time again, it often does not. In fact, life is not designed to turn out in a dualistic paradigm. I mean, just look around at what is happening with humanity. Look at the madness and suffering that the mind creates over and over again. Our problems cannot be solved at the level of consciousness from which we have created them. And certainly not if what is driving you is a sense of separation and compensation for not feeling you're good enough to begin with.

Even if you do happen to find yourself at the top of the pile, you soon realize that it's empty there too and that nothing outside one's self can bring the kind of happiness we all are truly looking for. Happiness is an inside job. It's one thing to have nothing and hate yourself. It is far worse to have the world admire you and to then realize that you *still* hate yourself. Ouch. That one is a real killer.

I sometimes think it was an angel in human form that paid me a visit that day in the jungle. I mean, what a gift that mysterious stranger gave to me. It had taken all those years, 20,000 dollars and all that hard work to finally live out what I thought was a dream come true. And though I did end up with an album full of my music, the realization that came with it that day when I was alone in the studio was priceless. I had let go of the music business and the idea of becoming a star just to please others. There was no one to prove anything to anymore, not even myself. I was a free man.

I could now find something in life that I wanted to do, for no other reason than for my own passion and satisfaction. In God's world there is nothing to prove. Only the ego is interested in looking good and being right. What you truly are has no need to prove anything. Why? Because we are already enough. We are everything we have always been looking for.

The process of letting go can sometimes come slowly or sometimes quickly. Most of my experience of letting go has simply been through the sheer agony of not being able to hold on anymore. It certainly hasn't been because of some intelligent wisdom or deep insight about what is happening in life. No. Most of the things that I have let go of have had fur and claw marks all over them. It is the attachment to things that creates suffering, because the very things we attach ourselves to are impermanent. Everything is on the way out, so why hold on to the illusion that it is not?

It was a physical act for me to finish that album but I also completed something emotionally. Most of us are not that well versed in completing. We're pretty good at starting and finishing things but completion is an art in itself. My guess is that there are a lot of emotionally incomplete people walking around. One might even say that the final journey is the ultimate completion of seeing through the illusion of opposites.

Now let me contradict myself once again here. Completion only takes place within the illusion of duality. In a state of absolute reality, there is no such thing as completion. When one emerges into a view of wholeness, there is nothing to complete. In fact there is nothing happening at all, nothing. This is a very difficult comment to comprehend as the mind cannot wrap itself around the fact that nothing is happening. The mind is responsible for making life look like things are happening, but no mind no happening.

And you know what? For some whacky reason we come into this world with the linear perception of duality. I have no idea why. Maybe it is karma, I don't know. You will have to talk to God about that one – and talking to God, in my experience, is by appointment only.

So that is the story of the magic in Mexico, the story of letting go of the past and completing the illusion of needing to prove myself to everyone. When I look back at the synchronicity of how it all happened, my mind literally boggles. This world we live in is truly a mystery. The more I know, the less I know, and that's all I know – if you know what I mean.

CHAPTER 9

Crazy Horse

"Everything you need to know about enlightenment is in everything, because everything is enlightened."

JC Mac

Crazy Horse, Sitting Bull and Black Elk all played a big part in the history of the Native American Lakota people. Crazy Horse was one of the warriors who took part in the battle of 'Little Big Horn,' the place where General Custer met his fate along with all of his men.

When he was young, Crazy Horse had a vision that told him to paint circles on his body and his horse when riding into battle, as this would protect him. He had such a deep belief in this vision that he did indeed become 'bulletproof.' It seemed to be impossible for anyone to kill him in battle. Sitting Bull was known for his leadership and was the chief of his people for many years. Black Elk was a renowned medicine man, who also had visions about the world and his people.

This brave tribe held out as long as they possibly could against the white man's plan to shift them onto the reservation. Here they would spend the rest of their days doing nothing but trying to survive. It is a tragic tale for such a proud and spirited group of people.

Some years ago, when I was living in London, I decided I wanted to put on a musical event. Well, more like a festival that was going to be in the grounds of this beautiful country estate, just outside of London. The whole thing was going to be based around the theme of world peace.

The idea was to bring bands and artists to play over a weekend and donate the money to a just cause. I also wanted a program of speakers; peacemakers from the United Nations, heads of tribes and key activists who were known for speaking out about world peace and the salvation of our planet. I decided that the profits from the event would go to different organizations, the ones that we all agreed could make a difference in the world today. So I began working on putting this whole thing together. I began to call up Buddhist monks, African chiefs, Indian gurus and so on, all of whom would share the stage with the musicians. Music, world peace and enlightenment all rolled into one. WOW.

During my time as a drug and alcohol counselor, I had worked with people from the Blackfoot and Lakota nations. Many were penniless, so they used to bring me eagle feathers as payment. When I left that place I had this huge fan of eagle feathers that were eventually beaded for me by an old medicine woman.

I had always been drawn to that spirit of the West and the Native Americans. For some reason, I have often felt Native American myself. So it seemed natural for me to get someone from that part of the world involved in our world peace and music event. So off I went searching the internet.

Before long, and through one of those divine synchronicities of life, I had the phone number of Chief Arvol Looking Horse, spiritual leader of over 50,000 Lakota on the Cheyenne River Reservation. I dialed the number and the next thing I knew I was speaking to the chief himself. It was the first number on a long list of people I wanted to invite to the event.

So there I was chatting away with Arvol about what I was planning to do. He said to me: "Well I won't answer whether I'll come or not until you come here and meet me. We will pray and chant in the sweat lodge, smoke the peace pipe, speak to the Great Spirit and then I'll let you know if I will be coming to your event." So the next day I jumped onto a plane and off I went to find the Lakota Chief. I flew to Denver and then drove to the reservation. When I finally arrived, it felt like I was coming home.

This was completely open country. There were no streets and Arvol didn't have an address as such. I just had to ask whoever I met where Arvol lived. People would just point in a direction and say: "That way." I would drive fifty miles at a time, and then ask someone again where the chief lived. These people had such a completely different way of doing and seeing things in the world. No GPS systems, no maps, and a very different concept of time. The spiritual relationship the Lakota had with life had no need for such technology.

After what seemed like forever, I eventually met with the chief, a tall, strikingly beautiful Lakota man with dark skin and hair that fell three quarters of the way down his back. Just what you would expect. (I mean, what a letdown it would have been to go all that way just to run into some fat, bald white man.)

It was horrible, however, to see just how much poverty there was amongst these gentle people. I thought it was disgusting that a man with that much pride would be forced into living like that and how so much had been taken from them.

We spent a lot of time just getting to know each other. Then, one clear summer's night, he took me out onto the plains where some of his people had set up a sweat lodge for us. I can still remember the magic of that Lakota night sky, full of stars. Everything around us was black; there were no city lights, no noise other then the sound of crickets chirping into the night. I felt incredibly blessed to be there with these magical people.

So, into the lodge we went to pray, sweat and smoke the pipe. I suddenly became aware that I participating in an ancient ceremony that has been practiced for thousands of years. Glowing hot rocks were brought in and dropped into a central pit. Animal hides covered the entire hut and entrance so there was no light and little oxygen. Sparks flew as we threw water into the deep pit and onto the rocks. We sweated and prayed four times, one for each direction: north, south, east and west.

There I was in the pitch black with Arvol and someone pounding on a drum, chanting my little heart out. It was the hottest place this white boy from the city had ever been. At one point I was lying on the floor looking for cracks through the animal skins to try and get some air. Thank God I was under cover of darkness and nobody could see me. It was an incredible experience.

THE ANATOMY OF A SPIRITUAL MELTDOWN

When the ceremony was over, we ran out of the tent, half naked with steam rising off us, and jumped straight into a freezing cold river. Shortly afterwards Arvol said he had spoken to the Great Spirit, and that it would be a good idea for him to attend the event. We headed back to Arvol's house and I slept like a baby as soon as my head hit the pillow.

I woke up with a huge smile on my face and a wonderfully warm sense of inner peace. I then stepped outside into a beautiful summer's morning. For as far as the eye could see, there was nothing but miles and miles of open plains stretched out before me. My mission had been a success. I was now on the road to producing a full-blown peace and music event.

The name 'Arvol Looking Horse' was given to the chief because of his ability to connect with wild horses that roamed freely throughout out the reservation. The Native Americans relate to all the animals on their land as having some kind of 'medicine' or power to bring insight and healing to humans and the planet. Arvol's magic was connecting with the power of the horse. He could walk out onto the open plains and these magnificent animals would appear, seemingly from nowhere, and gather around him. It was extraordinary to watch.

As for me, I was terrified of horses. I grew up in the city and so the biggest thing that I had ever seen was a dog or cat – or the occasional road kill. Nothing that matched the size of these beautiful animals. It wasn't that I'd ever had a bad experience with horses. I mean, I had never really been up close to one, but for some reason was scared of them. They just seemed so big and overpowering. These magnificent animals were far too terrifying for me to interact with and Arvol seemed to pick up on that. I was in awe of his ability to be so at home with them. It was as if he could speak to them and they could understand every word of what he was saying.

That very same morning, Arvol walked into the barn where all the horses were and began saddling one of them up. When he was finished I thought he had decided to go off for a ride so, in my ignorance, I began heading back to the house. As I did I heard his voice call out: "JC, mount up!" His hands were in the air pointing the reigns in my direction. Now, as you know by now, I have been in some touchy situations in my life. But the thought of climbing up onto that beast was terrifying. I mean point a gun at my head and I would be more relaxed than having to climb up on one of those animals. (Maybe I just had a dose of bad horse karma going on and it was payback time.)

My first response was to say: "No, it's OK Arvol. You go. I'll just hang around here until you get back." But he wasn't having any of it. "Mount up!" he insisted, in his Lakota twang. It was then that I realized he wasn't kidding. He really did want me to climb up onto that horse.

So there I was with the current chief of the Lakota nation saddling me up on the very thing in life that terrified me the most. I tried to explain just how scared I was of climbing onto this horse. He just said: "It will be OK. This horse is a gentle soul." So up I climbed onto my worst nightmare. Arvol slapped the horse on the backside and off I went into the wide blue yonder, clenching my teeth and hanging onto the reigns for dear life.

After a couple of minutes, I began to think to myself that this wasn't too bad after all. In fact, it was starting to feel something like fun. So, like a crazy fool, I thought I'd get him to run a little faster. In for a penny, in for a pound, as the English say. As we picked up speed, we started disappearing further out into the plains. I was so absorbed in this new experience that I wasn't keeping any track of how far away we had traveled from the barn.

As we continued, I started to think that I was really beginning to get the hang of this horse-riding thing. The scenery was stunning; the rolling plains of the Cheyenne River Reservation seemed to go on forever. I was breathing in the aroma of the tall grass and wild sage bushes. The sun was beating down on my face, the wind was in my hair and I was beginning to feel right at home. (Cue: Rawhide theme tune.) Thundering along on this magnificent horse was exhilarating.

That was not to last as I began to get the horrible feeling that I was starting to lose control – or what I thought was control. Panic rose in my chest and I began to pull on the leather reigns to get a handle on this horse, to try and steer him and slow him down a bit. But the horse was having none of it. He had no intention of doing anything I wanted him to do. I suddenly became horrified. I had no idea how to deal with an animal that big.

I was flying along in the middle of nowhere on the back of a horse that would not slow down. The harder I pulled on the reigns, the worse it got. I thought to myself: 'Sweet Jesus? I'm a dead man riding.' I truly believed that all I had managed to survive and accomplish during my short stay here on this planet was about to come to an end on the back of a horse. God really is a comedian.

And, wouldn't you know it? My worst nightmare did come true. The horse's front legs plunged deep into some kind of hole in the ground. When they did his legs buckled, and he fell forward onto his knees and the next thing I remember was my body hurtling headfirst through the air – and without the horse I might add.

At breakneck speed, and with very little grace, I barrel-rolled into space. The terrifying thought of just how painful the sudden stop was going to be – and how many of my bones were going to break – was overwhelming me. In short, I was screwed (and that's saying it lightly). It was time to pay the piper for all the misdeeds from my misspent youth. All that karma was finally coming back to pay me a visit.

Most prayers are just demands on God to get what we think we want in life – and in this case it was no different. With the remaining few seconds I had left, I began what I can only describe as 'speed begging': "Dear Lord," I pleaded, "just get me out of this one and I will never steal, swear, lie, cheat or act like an all round asshole ever again, I promise."

Thump. The next thing I was aware of was my feet planting themselves firmly on the ground. I stood there, perfectly upright, stunned and in shock. Wasn't I supposed to be dead, or horribly maimed?

I quickly checked my body for punctures, hemorrhaging and other fatal injuries. I couldn't believe that I was completely unscathed. The next thing I noticed was the horse, who by this time had obviously had enough of me, was galloping off into the distance.

I scanned the vast plains, wondering which way was home, and just where on earth that horse had bolted off to. Wherever home was, it looked like one hell of a walk without a ride. So I decided there was only one thing to do. No matter what it took, I had to get back up on that mount. It took me a good twenty minutes to eventually get my hands on the reigns and climb back up on top of that horse again.

It was crystal clear to me by now that there was no way I was ever going to force that animal to do anything. I needed to rethink my strategy of how I was going to get myself back in one piece. There was a head-scratching pause, then a voice inside me said: 'Stop trying to force things and just let go.' Aha!

It was at that moment that I surrendered to that magnificently powerful horse, and, as I did, he began to respond to me. I had now moved from a position of force to one of power, which has a completely different energy to it. Power is about allowing things to happen by influencing the universe with an intention of trust. Force, however, is about trying to bend life to your will. You see, there is God's will and then there is our will. Take a wild guess which one works better when it comes to having things turn out in life.

When I relaxed and allowed things just to happen, I somehow gave the horse the freedom to respond, instead of react to my fear-driven state. We were then both operating from the same place energetically. One might say (if this isn't too flaky for you) that the horse and I became one.

Instead of me thinking I could control the animal and make it do whatever I wanted it to do, we worked together to get back home. A gentle trusting pull here and there on the reigns produced much better results than all the desperate yanking and tugging that I had been doing earlier. The horse took the lead and trotted back home. He knew exactly how to get back.

When we eventually arrived at the stables, Arvol just took the saddle off and led the horse away. That was that. He didn't say much.

But I am sure that he knew on some level what was going on out there between me and that horse, or, as he would put it, between me and the Great Spirit. What a lesson in the art of letting go and letting God.

By the way the event ended up being cancelled but I still to this day remain in touch with those great Lakota warriors.

DEBRIEF

Force is linear and ego-based. It requires more and more strength and personal will. The harder you try, the harder it gets. You have to keep shoveling more and more coal into the furnace to keep it going. You can only keep this up for so long before you burn out. The more force you use, the more energy you need. Power on the other hand requires surrender and trust in the process of life. It requires letting go.

Take Ghandi for example. This man had no official 'authority' but, nevertheless, he managed to get the British colonial government to leave India. The British at that time, with all its military might and force, was no match for Ghandi. We spend most of our lives forcing things to turn out our way, instead of trusting in the power of divinity and letting that roll out the options in our lives. This does not mean we sit on our butts and do nothing. It means we take action without attachment to the outcome. We act and move on, letting go along the way. We become committed to life and at the same time unattached. With power, you have it; with force it has you.

My life has been all about *making* things happen. I always believed that if I just pushed hard enough, made enough contacts, talked people into things, I would, at some point, end up with what I wanted. My business career was driven by force. I clawed at the success food chain, pushing and pushing harder to get what I thought was going to make me happy.

My past had embedded in me that I alone had to make life work. I lived with an unconscious, underlying low-grade fear that if I didn't make it happen, nothing was going to happen. In essence I could not trust the process of life. Even with all the personal and spiritual development work I had done over the years, I still could not let go. In fact, it was my ego that wanted to become enlightened, and that, my friends, is an impossibility in reality. I now see that God's plan is much bigger than my little plans; if only I am willing to get out of the way.

THE ANATOMY OF A SPIRITUAL MELTDOWN

I was so wired for success that money and fame had become my god. I couldn't rest until I had reached the top of the heap. But the success came at a huge price. All that neurotic behavior, all that pushing and trying to bend life to my will started estranging me from my wife. Not only did my marriage break down, but I also lost my business, my home and even, for a while, access to my three children.

This was back in 2002 and it marked the beginning of the end of my ego's insistence on using force to get what it wanted in life. I reached a place where there was nothing left to do but surrender to life and all it was trying to teach me. When you rise to a new level of consciousness, you are left with the wreckage from the level below it.

The Buddha once said: "There is only one sin and that is the sin of ignorance." If that is the case, then I was one ignorant son of a bitch.

The horse showed me, yet again, that I am not running the show and that the sooner I accept life on life's terms, the sooner I will live in peace. Why did the horse respond to me the way it did on the way home? My guess, because the horse knew more about the nature of reality than me.

CHAPTER 10

Final Comments

All the lessons I have shared with you in this book I have learned the hard way. My hope is that you can take what I offered in this little book and use it to learn the nature of reality in a softer, gentler way.

There are many ways up a mountain. These stories point to just some of those ways. Learn from my mistakes and turn that knowledge into wisdom. There is no need to be as stubborn and ignorant as I have been, in order to have the state known as enlightenment to spontaneously emerge. It could happen while you are walking down the street one day, taking a bath, driving a car, or, as in my case, hanging up the phone.

The trick is to know that all of existence is influencing all of existence, and when conditions are appropriate, potentiality emerges as an actuality. Good karma (cause and effect in the world of duality) does not lead to enlightenment. It may improve your conditions in life but until you see your own true nature (that you are already enlightened), the wheel of rebirth and death keeps turning – and humanity keeps on suffering.

For many of us, the road to heaven starts in hell. Everything in the way of your realization of what you truly are has to be overcome – and that journey is not for the weak of heart. If it were easy, you would see so many more walking the streets having broken through the barrier of duality.

There is no magic pill that can have you transcend the ego. It is all a lot of work for most of us. It has been a lifetime's struggle for me. I have never seen anyone become enlightened through meditation, religion, reading books or performing some kind of mystical ritual. It may contribute to improving the conditions towards that state, depending on your intentions, but nothing *causes* enlightenment to happen. It emerges when the obstacles to its view are removed. In fact, from my research all enlightened people say the same thing:

THE ANATOMY OF A SPIRITUAL MELTDOWN

'Stop searching. You are already that which you seek. You are already enlightened.' In fact, most people who are enlightened don't actually see it as anything particularly special. What is insane is *not* being enlightened.

As I mentioned earlier, overcoming the obstacles in the way of transcending duality can be a very painful ride. It is a tough call to be confronted with having to surrender and let go of everything. The illusions you hang onto are often like thorns in your side, except they have been there so long you are scared to pull them out. Instead, you just learn to live with them.

I personally feel that most of us have been deluded by the 'spiritual circus.' The business of enlightenment, of ultimate happiness, has been turned into an industry. There is someone in every bookstore, or on every corner, trying to sell you their way, as the only way. In my opinion, most of this is, as they say in Texas, 'just a load of gun smoke and horseshit.'

The shelves are full of self-help and 'how to' books proclaiming they have the answer to almost every problem the ego can come up with. That is just the blind leading the blind. You have as much chance of realizing the state of enlightenment by eating pizza one day as you do living in a monastery or following a charismatic guru.

I keep telling people to stop trying to become enlightened. They think it is a place to get to but it is not. It has no location in time or space. So how in the world could you get there by searching relentlessly for its front door? There are gurus who will tell you anything to make you believe they are the answer. There are all kinds of self-proclaimed experts on the subject of how to become enlightened who preach that all you need to do is follow them. Don't believe it for a moment. This is a cunning ego at work.

In all my years on this path, I have met only a couple of truly enlightened people and they don't even want anyone following them around. They are just not interested, as what they have become is more than enough to raise the consciousness of the world.

This ride, if you are strong enough, is taken between you and God and no one else. So watch what you pray for. You just might get it.

I love you all…

JC Mac